EUROPE'S ESTABLISHED AND EMERGING IMMIGRANT COMMUNITIES

IMMIGRANT COMMUNITIES

assimilation, multiculturalism or integration

EUROPE'S ESTABLISHED AND EMERGING IMMIGRANT COMMUNITIES

assimilation, multiculturalism or integration

*Edited by Carlton Howson
and Momodou Sallah*

Trentham Books

Stoke on Trent, UK and Sterling, USA

Trentham Books Limited

Westview House   22883 Quicksilver Drive

734 London Road Sterling

Oakhill   VA 20166-2012

Stoke on Trent   USA

Staffordshire

England ST4 5NP

First published 2009

British Library Cataloguing-in-Publication Data
A catalogue record for this book is available from the British Library

ISBN: 978 1 85856 466 1

Thanks to Soft Touch Art for the cover picture. It comes from the Arrived! project in which the participatory arts organisation Soft Touch Arts worked with young people newly arrived in Leicester to make a magazine about themselves and their experiences. The two young men in the photo are unaccompanied young asylum seekers from Afghanistan. One of them captioned this photo 'I came to England because in Afghanistan everyone is fighting'.

Designed and typeset by Trentham Books Ltd and printed in Great Britain by Page Bros (Norwich) Ltd, Norfolk.

Contents

Dedication

This book is dedicated to the people who have contributed to making it happen. It acknowledges the efforts of those who have gone before and those who continue with the audacity of hope, as we recognise difference as a reality and work to attain security where people are not treated inhumanly on account of difference.

Carlton Howson and Momodou Sallah

Introduction

Momodou Sallah and Carlton Howson

Introduction

The origins of this book can be traced to a growing concern over the relationship between white European people who are not subjected to the brutality of imperialism, and Black ethnically minoritised people. It draws on research and the experiences of academics and practitioners who attempt to reflect the experiences and stories of people they work with. The book takes a multi-disciplinary and multi-faceted approach to the construction and enaction of 'difference', especially in relation to established and emerging immigrant communities, with a view to attracting attention from diverse fields of study. The book was inspired by a conference that took place in November 2007, with the same title as this book, that brought together experts, practitioners and academics to discuss pertinent issues on this theme. Many of the participants welcomed the opportunity to discuss a range of issues relevant to Europe's established and emerging immigrant communities, such as health, policing, refuge and asylum seekers, education, housing, integration/cohesion and terrorism. The level of interest prompted us to put this publication together.

The book argues that many of the state attempts at integrating different social groups have failed and that this failure is due to state policy where 'race' has proved to be one of the most enduring signifiers of status, acceptance, rejection and exclusion. In recent years, race and faith have become amalgamated as the state attempts to justify its ongoing invasions and imperialistic attacks, invoking catastrophic horror on ordinary people here and abroad, whilst simultaneously observing other abuses of human rights. The devastation caused has become embedded and is part of people's consciousness; yet a great number of people lack the understanding of why they are so alienated, why they hold the feelings they do about their neighbours. Race continues to invoke feelings of hostility between groups and the state with its various instruments still manipulates people. This is the picture not only in one state but in many states across Europe; hence the exploration of the various chapters in the book.

It is divided into two parts: the first looks mainly at specific situations that are acted across more than one state and sometimes right across Western Europe. The second explores scenarios particular to the UK but relevant to other parts of Europe as well.

In Chapter 1, Sallah introduces us to themes of how Europe addresses the question of migrants, arguing that migrants and their descendents continue to be regarded as 'others'. He explores some of the contradictions as played out in a number of European countries and concludes that Europe is no longer what it was and not yet what it will be; the dawn of a new Europe calls for a recalibration of the understanding of the complexities Europe is confronted with.

In Chapter 2, Ramadan challenges our conceptualisation of the use of the term 'immigrants'. He argues for a clear distinction between those Muslims who *were* immigrants 50 years ago and the more recent experience of people who are Muslims but who are not immigrants. He maintains that a silent revolution is taking place as a reaction to outdated policies that divide people into hostile camps, Islamic and non-Islamic, and argues that we have a shared responsibility to move toward a 'revolution of trust and confidence, of critical loyalty' and the 'birth of a new we'.

In Chapter 3, Johnson points out that whilst there is much diversity within Europe, there is also considerable convergence and consistency in research findings about the health and welfare needs of ethnic groups across Europe. He shows that social policy and the response to migrants have been discriminatory and unhealthy, and suggests that health and migration are a global phenomenon that requires an urgent global response to avoid the mistakes of the past.

In Chapter 4, Dyson identifies a new signifier for the 'new Europe'; he draws on his experience and research on sickle cell to explore how a more diverse Europe presents challenges in terms of how we think of ourselves and others. He believes that we should embrace difference as an alternative, suggesting that conflation of ethnic groups, colour or ethnic blindness is a signifier of cultural incompetence and can have devastating outcomes for health care. We need a model that signifies both our connectedness *and* our difference.

In Chapter 5, Phillimore explores how government policy in Europe has largely sought to deter people from seeking asylum in Europe. Measures taken have proved restrictionist and anti-integration for both those seeking asylum and those who have been granted leave to remain. These policies perpetuate the notion of 'undeserving', thereby absolving the state of its responsibilities whilst subjecting such groups to further exclusion.

In Chapter 6, Valentine, Sporton and Nielson look at specific examples of Somali refugee and asylum seekers in the UK and Denmark; and how the different policy contexts affect their integration in the respective countries. The chapter also reflects on how identities are formed based on the narratives of those participating in the research. It continues themes raised earlier and illustrates how attempts by refugee and asylum seekers to fit in are disrupted by the process of being 'othered' or regarded as strangers.

In Chapter 7, Grattan, Zhunich and McMullan draw attention to the fragility of some relationships of people in Northern Island and Bosnia Herzegovina and how social, political and economic pressures have contributed to the eruption that led to the breakdown between groups that formerly lived together. The consequences include increased segregation and separation, nationalism, ethnocentric and xenophobic violence. Therefore youth and community work must engage not only with the local community history and tradition but also with the influence of modern globalism.

In Chapter 8, Brown focuses on England but makes reference also to other western European countries. He highlights the tensions between host and migrant communities, suggesting that community cohesion may be harder to attain in rural areas. He concludes that there is an urgent need to tackle inadequate housing conditions and the poor quality of life faced by excluded groups such as Travellers, Gypsies and migrant workers.

In Chapter 9 Stanislas explores how new Polish and Somalian migrants view British policing and asks whether the impact of British society shapes how these groups perceive policing. Polish and Somalian communities in Britain both experience a great deal of hostility and this operates at the level of ethnicity and gender. Stanislas concludes that the police service needs to reflect on how it undertakes its duties in response to the dominant host society and whether this differs for new and existing ethnic minority communities.

Howson in Chapter 10 considers some recent and historical struggles for inclusion, using higher education as a site of struggle in the sense that education is still seen as one of the most effective means of allocating social position whilst challenging discrimination. He argues that Black and ethnic minority people are manipulated in a manner that intensifies difference. Moreover, far from challenging discrimination, higher education nurtures it and the engagement and attainment levels of Black and ethnically minori-tised and white working class people are achieved in spite of, rather than because of initiatives such as widening participation.

In Chapter 11, Richardson questions whether a multiculturalist approach exists in relation to policies aimed at Gypsies and Travellers. She argues that even though Gypsies and Travellers are recognised as an ethnic group (Race Relations Act 1976), they continue to be excluded. This chapter extends the chapters by Brown and others by considering specifically how inadequate provision increases hostility and sustains the notion of 'other'; leaving Gypsies and Travellers with only two options: assimilation or exclusion.

In Chapter 12 Thomas explores whether community cohesion policy sig-nalled the death of multiculturalism. He traces the popularisation of com-munity cohesion in the UK back to the disturbances of 2001 and the notion of 'parallel lives' and concludes that community cohesion is another phase of multiculturalism.

Carlton Howson and Momodou Sallah
November 2009

1

Dawn of a new Europe: addressing 'otherness'

Momodou Sallah

Introduction

Although the construction of 'otherness' in Europe is seldom clear-cut, the demographic changes in Europe over the past 50 years and their consequences call for a recalibrated understanding of how minorities, often perceived as different and 'other', are treated. The central argument of this chapter is that, as a consequence of the rapid and still ongoing demographic changes over the last 50 years, Europe continues to construct parts of its body as different and 'other'; sometimes even denying citizenship through institutional and structural means to 'otherised' communities. The chapter starts by exploring how Europe has changed over the last 50 years and how 'otherness' has been constructed, enacted and internalised. It explores the often exploited argument that 'immigrants are taking over', and also the vitriolic rhetoric of the Far Right. This is juxtaposed with the incessant knocking on the doors of fortress Europe by immigrants who come in little boats from somewhere in Sub-Saharan Africa. The denial of citizenship and the management of difference are explored in relation to the changing demographics and the emergence of a multicultural Europe which demands that culturally competent services be provided to all its inhabitants.

Although about Europe, the chapter is largely limited to Western Europe. So the variety of European histories, national constitution, ethnic composition, political and socio-economic dispensation and numerous other factors make it almost impossible to speak of a homogeneous European experience; the exploration of these complexities are beyond the scope of this chapter. But it is intended as the background against which the rest of the chapters are painted and attempts to find the common denominator – the response to the construction of 'otherness'.

Changing demographics

'Established' and emerging immigrant communities continue to form a significant percentage of the population of European countries. Poland (2%) and Romania (0.5) have the lowest number of immigrants in Europe. Many have much higher proportions, with Andorra topping them all with 77 per cent of its 82,000 inhabitants being immigrants. Immigrants make up 70 per cent of Monaco's population of 32,000; and 37 per cent of Luxembourg's 480,000. So the smaller countries have a far larger proportion who can be classified as immigrants or 'foreign born'. However, the bigger European countries also have significant immigrant populations: 23 per cent of Switzerland's 7.5 million people are described as foreign born, Austria 15 per cent, Ireland 14 per cent, Germany 12 per cent, Sweden 12 per cent, Italy 11 per cent, Spain 11 per cent, France 10 per cent, the Netherlands 10 per cent and the UK 9 per cent. Also important is the origin of the immigrants. Of the 3.5 million people who settled in the EU27 in 2006, 86 per cent were foreigners and 1.8 million of the immigrants came from outside the EU, with Morocco the leading country of origin. The volume of migration has been steadily increasing since 1990: the number who came to Europe in 1990 was 49.4 million. There were 55.3 million in 1995, 58.2 million in 2000 and 64.1 million in 2005 (Eurostat, 2008; UN Department of Economic and Social Affairs Population Division, 2006).

Tensions around difference

In the forums around diversity and difference and among many of my colleagues who work in the diversity field, the preferred terms are often soft-core: intercultural competence, community cohesion, and cultural awareness. Terms like oppression, anti-discriminatory practice and anti-racism seem to worry officialdom. We encounter a culture of denial, where people who have not experienced discrimination cannot even begin to conceptualise discrimination, let alone understand its structural and internalised impact. They bury their heads in the sand, shut their eyes and cover their ears, chanting; 'I see no evil, I hear no evil' whilst their arses are on fire. Difference is not a universal conceptualisation; it is located within individual and collective experiences of demarcation and such boundaries can be manifested differently. The next section explores four examples of difference which erupted into violence and tension.

The Danish cartoons

When a Danish newspaper, *Jyllands-Posten*, printed caricatures of the prophet Muhammad in 2005, it sparked an upheaval. Muslims not only in Denmark but all over the world felt that their prophet had been subjected to ridicule and disrespect (*Times*, 31.1.2006). A significant proportion of Danish society and of the West felt that the Muslim protests were an attempt to stifle freedom of speech and censor the press, and thus violated Western democracy (Pipes, 2006). Complicating this picture, however, was the fact that some people caught up in the conflict were both Danish/European citizens and Muslims. To what extent does one owe allegiance to Danish citizenship while also following the dictates of one's religion? To what extent does the Danish state or any other Western European government accommodate or otherised citizens in mainstream spaces? These were the fundamental tensions the Danish cartoon incident threw up. Can one be European and also other, in this case Muslim?

The French riots

The second wave of the riots in France in January 2006 were linked largely to the collective opposition of the First Employment Contract. This in turn was linked to vulnerability to job insecurity, protecting the rights of workers and countering lower wages. The protesters/rioters were mainly white youths (Sahlins, 2006). The earlier riots of November 2005 began after two French young people of Tunisian and Malian origin were electrocuted whilst being pursued by the French police in the Parisian suburb of Clichy-sous-Bois.

For about three weeks after their deaths, there were severe riots in many parts of Paris. About 274 towns experienced rioting, largely involving second and third generation unemployed 'immigrant citizens'. Paradoxically, whilst most of these young people hold French nationality and many have never known any other home, they are sometimes labelled and treated as immigrants. This trend is not unique to France and can be observed in a significant number of European countries. An estimated 9000 cars and dozens of public buildings were burnt, and many rioters fought running battles with the police. Sahlins (2006) observed that:

> In fact while most of the rioters were second generation immigrant youths, the underlying issues were far more complex, involving social and economic exclusion, racial discrimination, and most importantly the capacity of the French Republic to respond to these challenges while maintaining its distinctive model of and formal commitment to the social integration of individuals, no matter their colour or creed.

The crucial issue is how 'immigrant citizens,' especially the young, are excluded and otherised. How much do they feel they belong and where else can they find a sense of significance, solidarity and security (Clark, 1996)? And perhaps most importantly, how does their *construction* as 'immigrants' and as 'others' affect their life chances in French society?

Theo van Gough's assassination

The assassination of Theo van Gogh in November 2004 by a 26 year-old man of Moroccan origin highlighted the tension in Dutch society between established and emerging immigrant communities and mainstream society. One reaction to the assassination was that critical questions were raised about the place of immigrants in Dutch society. The electoral success of List Pim Fortuyn in 2002 arguably instigated a political shift in which the established political parties in Holland, including the Socialist Party, began to adopt more restrictionist policies towards immigration. This stance contradicted the social liberalism with which Dutch society has traditionally been associated. The political shift manifested in such events as the deportation of 26,000 immigrants, some of them long-standing residents, in rapidly-conducted proceedings, and the new requirement for immigrants to take Dutch language classes, paid for from their own pockets.

However, the fact that a significant number of 'immigrants/immigrant citizens' endure deprivation and exclusion can easily be overlooked. Unemployment among immigrants was four times above the national average and 40 per cent of all foreigners were leaving school before completing their final exams. The assassination of van Gough has highlighted some of the tensions of managing difference and the plight of Dutch immigrants. A young Dutch girl of Moroccan origin captures this tension well:

> When I hear people talk about 'those fucking Moroccans,' I feel defensive and really want to be Moroccan, but when I visit Morocco I know I don't belong there, either. (A young Moroccan girl, quoted in Buruma, 2005)

July 2001: The British 'Summer of Unrest'

The 2001 riots in the Northern cities of England – principally in Bradford, Oldham and Burnley – were largely confrontations between British youths of South Asian origin and British white youths. They resulted in numerous injuries and significant damage to property. Cantle (2001) diagnosed that the communities were living 'parallel lives': going to different schools, attending different places of worship, having different socialisation spaces and therefore with no intersection in their lives, even when they did share the same post codes. In 2005, Phillips argued that Britain was 'sleepwalking into segregation' by continuing to promote a multicultural approach which, he maintained, segregated communities. This has been countered by Kudnani (2007) who has pointed to the success of multiculturalism.

What emerged from the South Asian youths was that they felt they were subjected to state sanctioned, institutionalised discriminatory and exclusionary practices. They were 'otherised' because they were constructed as 'immigrants,' even though most had been born in England and hold British citizenship.

These are just four of many scenarios that illustrate the tensions surrounding the new forms of European identity being negotiated and forged. Ramadan (2007) postulates this as a process of Europe undergoing an 'identity crisis' in which the constructions of 'normality' and the social spaces for action and interaction are shifting; moving against the prevailing dominant mainstream values and 'reality' which defines the 'symbolic universe' (Berger and Luckman, 1966). The four events discussed also illustrate the demarcation of the boundary between 'Europeans' and the 'other' as the frontline. The boundary, however, pays little respect to the distinctions and variations of otherness regardless of citizenship status.

Immigration into Europe has been driven by a variety of reasons that have changed over time. Historically speaking, immigration into Europe has always existed (Bade, 2003; Fryer, 1984). A huge chunk of Europe's population are not indigenes but are themselves descendents of immigrants. We therefore use the phrase 'established and emerging immigrant communities' with some reservation. It has discriminatory connotations, but there is no unproblematic phrase that encapsulates the section of the population we refer to.

A significant wave of immigration to Europe in the twentieth century was driven by the need for labour after the Second World War, and the active recruitment of people from South Asia, Latin America, Africa and the Caribbean. Other subsequent drivers of immigration have included the pursuit of high-status education among those in former colonies, the rights of former colonial subjects to settle in European countries, and the claiming of refuge and asylum by people from areas of disaster and conflict such as Uganda, Montserrat, Somalia and Rwanda.

Whatever the reason for migration, which is unique to each individual country, immigration to Europe steadily increases. Whilst this chapter is being written, thousands of young people from all over the world are trying to enter European countries. This often entails extremely perilous journeys and detention in grim conditions. Whatever their motivation for immigration, there has been a huge rise in the number of those who can be constructed as 'others', especially because of their colour and culture. These 'others' now constitute a significant portion of the population, and include citizens of Europe, long term residents, and newly arrived communities.

Little boats from across the ocean: Berca or berserk!

The conceptual dichotomy 'Berca or Berserk!' has been immortalised in several Senegalese rap songs. It embodies the idea that the socio-economic and political conditions in some sub-Saharan African countries make life so intolerable that their residents are left with only two choices: either do every-thing in their power to enter Europe, including crossing the ocean to Spain (symbolised by Berca – i.e. Barcelona) in fragile little canoes or go to 'berserk' and face oblivion, nothingness, the hereafter. That is, either get into Europe and improve one's station in life or die trying! DJ Awadi, a popular Senegalese rap artist, captures this in his popular song *Sunugal* (our boat):

> You had promised me that I would have a job
> You had promised me that I would never be hungry
> You had promised me true activities and a future
> Really up to here I still see nothing
> That's why I decided to flee, that's why I break myself in dugout (canoe)
> I swear it ! I can't stay here one more second.
> It is better to die than to live in such conditions, in this hell
> Come what may
> I again prefer to die
> The political journalists are in prison or in the DIC (Criminals Investigations Department)
> The political opponents are in prison or in the DIC
> Too many companies are bankrupt
> ICS, SONACOS all sink into the bankruptcy.
> Every day your scandals flood our radios
> (DJ Awadi, online)

What it is that drives young people to undertake life-threatening journeys deserve better attention. Such issues include not only the corrupt governance by some African leaders but also the colonial legacy. Sustained unfair struc-tures, principally orchestrated by the Brettonwoods institutions through un-fair trade practices, keeps a significant number of sub-Saharan African coun-tries submerged in poverty. Gross injustice and global inequality are propped up by undemocratic and unaccountable structures like the IMF, World Bank and the WTO (Milanovic, 1999; UNDP, 2005; *New Internationalist,* 2004).

This pattern of going to Europe, whilst to some extent ameliorative, is not the magic silver bullet: sub-Saharan Africa received only 1.5 per cent of all remittance flows in 2002 (UNFPA, 2006). While unfair practices persist, poverty and destitution will drive people to the mantra of Berca or Berserk. And this means there is a continuous fight over the attempts of people to enter fortress Europe. Morever for those who do penetrate Europe, whether legally or illegally, the perception and management of their difference remains a site of contestation.

The white working class and the Far Right's accusations

Nick Griffiths, leader of the Far Right British National Party and recently elected MEP has called for boats carrying would-be immigrants from the Sahara into Spain to be sunk so as to act as a deterrent to further migration:

> Frankly, they need to sink several of those boats ...They can throw them a life-raft and they can go back to Libya. But Europe has sooner or later to close its borders or it's simply going to be swamped by the Third World. (*The Scotsman*, 9.7. 2009)

Parties of the Far Right are gaining political support across Europe, especially during this period of economic decline which creates fertile ground for the germination of such ideology. What is sometimes missed from the discourse is that in their own concept of social reality, some white working class people have rational fears of being excluded and even 'discriminated against.' The accommodation of those considered 'others' in social housing and the scarcity of secure employment in many areas fuel these perceptions. So subjective marginalisation of some poor white working class communities warrants attention too. It has much to do with class and deprivation; a similar situation to that of most minorities. A common denominator made up of class, deprivation and discrimination. The spreading of the Far Right, built largely on the whipping up of resentment, must be a legitimate part of the discussion and their messages must be logically dismantled.

Construction, enaction and internalisation of otherness – race and ethnicity

Certain events have strengthened the boundary between Europeans and 'others,' be they established or emerging immigrant communities. The scale of immigration into Europe over the last 50 years is unprecedented. It is partly because of globalisation, which has made the movement of people much easier. But paradoxically, never before has such a solid fortress based on the exclusion of others been built around Europe to stop the others from coming in. And the 'others' who are already here, even though they might be second or third generation are treated differently because of their otherness. The tensions caused by otherness raises questions about how British citizens of South Asian origin felt they were treated by the state because of their ethnic origin, and questions about socio-economic parity with the rest of the population. One response was the summer of unrest in 2001.

The French approach to dealing with difference, however, is rooted in its colonial legacy of assimilation. This was based on the principle of turning all its colonial subjects into French men and women who think, talk, eat, sleep and even go to the toilet like French men and women. It characterises the present approach in France to managing established and emerging immigrant communities: difference cannot be enacted in the public sphere. The widely publicised banning of Muslim headscarves and other religious symbols in 2004 is just the tip of the iceberg. Recent utterances by Sarkozy about the niqab and burka as symbols of Muslim women being subjugated are more revealing (*Guardian*, 22/06/09). The French riots were driven by the deep-seated frustration of 'immigrant' youths in France who felt treated like second class citizens because they fared worse than the average French citizen regarding housing, employment, education and social mobility.

In the case of Denmark, it can be argued that the Danish cartoons were just a manifestation of deeper socio-economic issues due to Danish citizens of immigrant backgrounds, especially Muslims, not feeling respected or justly treated. This has to be balanced against the desire of the 'indigenes' to preserve one of the fundamental tenets of Western democracy – freedom of speech. Again the fundamental conflict went beyond religion: it revolved around how an expanding population, who were once numerically insignificant, have now become so significant that they can no longer be ignored, especially given Europe's aging population (Carone and Costello, 2006). In the UK, Leicester, Bradford and Birmingham are projected to be the first cities to have ethnic minorities as their majorities; the same trend can be noted in European cities like parts of Paris and Amsterdam. This calls for recalibrations to approaches to difference.

The aftermath of the assassination of Theo van Gough revealed the deep-seated tensions existing in not only Holland in terms of the actions of an extremist, but also and especially the underlying tensions caused by deprivation, discrimination and the devaluation of the 'others' construction of social reality. Inextricably linked to the management of difference and otherness is the growing success of the Far Right and the disaffection of some white working class people who experience similar deprivation to that experienced by the established and emerging immigrant communities.

We are aware of the various approaches to managing difference; for example Britain's flirtation with multiculturalism in the 80s and 90s and its eventual marriage to *Integration* after the bombings of 7.7.2005. Equally the enforcement of assimilation since the days of colonialism in France has not changed much despite its massive increase in immigrants. Generally, the approach to managing difference and diversity is unique to each country.

Dawn of a new Europe

Europe, then, is not what it used to be, yet it is not what it will be. Old constructions of 'normality' and 'reality' are being deconstructed – the process of development is not static but dynamic. In most Western European countries, the birth rates of the majority populations continue to decline whilst those of the ethnic minority populations rise. The various demarcations between indigenes and others sometimes effected personally and structurally, that otherise and disadvantage immigrant communities in social, economic, political, cultural and faith spheres concern:

- the health needs of established and emerging immigrant communities in relation to issues like diabetes and sickle cell
- the faith and cultural needs such as wearing the hijab and requiring mosques in the neighbourhood
- the economic considerations created because established and emerging immigrant communities are more vulnerable to unemployment and underemployment
- the educational needs that arise when emerging immigrants' cultural location and construction of the self are discarded and stereotypes are imposed.
- Young people's negotiation of competing identities.

All these demand urgent attention. They should be sensitively managed to ensure that Europe is not consumed by conflict from within. It is these pressing issues that the rest of the book addresses. Whilst we cannot claim to have covered every issue exhaustively, we do hope that this book becomes a catalyst for greater debate and discussion that will lead to action.

References

Awadi (2008) *Sunugal* http://www.studiosankara.com/sunugaal.html http://medilinkz.org/news/news2.asp?NewsID=17717 (Senegalese Youth migration) Access 22/07/09

Bade, KJ (2003) *Migration in European History.* Oxford: Blackwell Publishing

Berger, P and Luckman, T. (1966) *The Social Construction of Reality: A treatise in the sociology of Knowledge.* Harmondsworth, Penguin

Buruma, I (2005) Letter from Amsterdam Final Cut After a filmmaker's murder, the Dutch creed of tolerance has come under siege. January 3, 2005 http://www.newyorker.com/archive/2005/01/03/050103fa_fact1?currentPage=1 Accessed 4/08/09

Cantle, T (2001) *Community Cohesion – A Report of the Independent Review Team.* London: Home Office

Carone, G and Costello, D (2006) Can Europe Afford to Grow Old? *Finance and Development* (A quarterly magazine of the IMF) September 2006, Volume 43, Number 3

Clark, D (1996) *Schools as Learning Communities.* London: Cassell

Eurostat (2008) Recent migration trends: citizens of EU-27 Member States become ever more mobile while EU remains attractive to non-EU citizens http://epp.eurostat.ec.europa.eu/cache/ITY_OFFPUB/KS-SF-08-098/EN/KS-SF-08-098-EN.PDF Accessed 22/07/09

Fryer, P (1984) *Staying Power: Black people in Britain.* London: Pluto Press

Guardian (2009) Nicolas Sarkozy says Islamic veils are not welcome in France http://www.guardian.co.uk/world/2009/jun/22/islamic-veils-sarkozy-speech-france Accessed 4/08/09

Kundnani, A (2007) *The End of Tolerance: Racism in 21st Century Britain.* London: Pluto Press

Milanovic, B (1999) 'True world income distribution, 1988 and 1993 – first calculations, based on household surveys alone,' *Policy Research Working Paper Series* 2244, The World Bank

New Internationalist (2004) IMF/World Bank: the facts Issue, 365, pp1 -7

Phillips, T (2005): After 7/7: Sleepwalking to segregation. Speech given at the Manchester Council for Community Relations, 22nd September 2005. Available at: http://www.cre.gov.uk/Default.aspx.LocID-0hgnew07s.RefLocID-0hg00900c002.Lang-EN.htm

Pipes, D (2006) Cartoons and Islamic Imperialism. *New York Sun* 7. 2. 2006

Ramadan, T. (2007) Keynote speech delivered at the Europe and Its Established and Emerging Immigrant Communities Conference held at De Montfort University, 10-11 November 2007

Sahlins, P (2006) Civil Unrest in the French Suburbs, November 2005. Available at: http://riotsfrance.ssrc.org/ Accessed:4/08/9

The Scotsman. BNP leader says 'sink boats to stop migrants' 9. 7. 2009

The Times (2006) Denmark faces international boycott over Muslim cartoons. 31.1.2006. accessed from: http://www.timesonline.co.uk/tol/news/world/europe/article723266.ece 22/07/09

UN Department of Economic and Social Affairs Population Division (2006) *Part One: International Migration Levels, Trends and Policies* http://www.un.org/esa/population/publications/2006_MigrationRep/part_one.pdf Accessed 22/07/09

UNFPA (2006) *A Passage to Hope: Women and International Migration.* UNFPA

PART 1

2

Muslims and European policies: the way forward

Tariq Ramadan

Over the past 20 years a profound change has taken place among the younger generation of Muslims in Europe. Fifty years ago most Muslims were immigrants who came looking for work and planned to return home as soon as they could. For the most part, this first generation came from simple backgrounds. They had made no great study of Islam and continued religious practices that remained heavily marked by their culture of origin, whether Indo-Pakistani, North African or Turkish.

Assuming that their stay was temporary, parents at first tried to protect themselves from this unfamiliar European environment rather than integrate themselves into it. But most of these original immigrants never left. Their children were born in Europe, became fluent in their national language and became better educated than their elders. The parents' dream of going home faded. The emergence of this new generation of European Muslims has resulted in a new way of thinking and talking about the nature of Islamic communities here.

Silent Revolution

Now a silent revolution is taking place. Old concepts that divided the world into two hostile camps, Islamic versus non-Islamic, are outdated and have been reviewed. European constitutions allow Muslims to practice their religion and should therefore be respected. Religious principles should not be confused with culture of origin: European Muslims should only be Muslim instead of forever remaining North African, Pakistani or Turkish Muslims.

Active citizenship is encouraged and a European Islamic culture needs to be created by respecting Islamic principles while adopting European tastes and styles.

Mentalities are changing fast. Islamic associations are active at the local level, building bridges and encouraging Muslim citizens to vote. New artistic voices are being heard. Although this energy and vitality are particularly visible in countries with the oldest Muslim presence, the same phenomenon is also underway elsewhere. But numerous challenges remain and the day when Muslims and their fellow-citizens can live together in harmony is still far-off. A series of stumbling blocks exist within Muslim communities that need to be reformed.

Too many Muslims are getting things mixed up. Problems of discrimination in housing or the workplace should not be taken as attacks on Islam but as the effects of social policies that we must commit ourselves to changing, as citizens demanding equal rights. Muslims must not fall into a victim mentality and the alibi that Islamophobia is preventing them from flourishing. It's up to Muslims to assume their responsibilities, construct clear arguments, engage in dialogue both within their own communities and with other fellow citizens and reject the simplistic vision of 'us versus them.'

Muslims should promote common values of equality, justice and respect in the name of a shared 'ethic of citizenship'. Over time they must do away with the temptation to shut themselves off as an isolated minority: otherwise they encourage those extremist voices that argue 'You are more Muslim when you're against the West'. The Muslims of Europe must be more self-critical.

Fellow citizens

Their non-Muslim fellow citizens need to make an effort too. They need to accept that Europe's population has changed, that it no longer has a single history and that the future calls for mutual understanding and respect. They need to face up to their ignorance and reject the clichés and prejudices that surround Islam. They must start discussing the principles, values and forms that will enable us to live together. The new Muslim presence poses a series of unavoidable questions to all the citizens of Europe. Are you prepared to study the history of a civilisation that is present in your lives and which forms part of your pluralistic society? Do you sincerely believe that Muslims – with their spirituality, ethics and creativity – have a positive contribution to make?

The future of Europe, with a flourishing Muslim presence and an open European identity, will be built by all those who accept this challenge. It will be based on self-criticism, lasting and demanding dialogue, respect for diversity and the expression of common values. The path leads from simple integration to mutual enrichment. It will take time and, above all it means that we are going to have to start trusting each other.

Challenges

The presence of millions of European Muslims raises a series of questions that are being asked in each country: Are Muslim citizens about to change our culture and our traditions? Are our Greco-Roman and Judaeo-Christian values under threat? How do we define and protect our identity? With its long history of welcoming immigrants and due to the nature of its Muslim population, European societies are at the forefront in addressing these issues, as well as in putting forward new answers that are emerging from these Western Muslim communities.

It is important to begin by specifying the fundamental nature of the problem: the increased visibility of Muslims in European societies is leading towards a genuine crisis of identity. As old reference points disappear it becomes harder to believe that Muslims can be fully European. A feeling of confusion has emerged amongst ordinary people, oscillating between doubt over their ability to preserve their culture and fear of being invaded by the customs and values of the other: the European citizens with a Muslim background. Doubt and fear commonly provoke reactions of shutting out or of rejection, both of which characterise an identity crisis.

Fears and identities

European Muslims need to pay more attention to the doubts and fears of their fellow citizens. They should realise that their fellow citizens, who are not Muslims, are not comfortable with the way that Muslims define themselves, including their own relationship with Islam. While the general atmosphere is full of suspicion, Muslims have a duty to establish intellectual, social, cultural and political spaces for the development of trust and appeasement.

This has to begin with an engagement in a clear discussion about Islam, about the practices and the values that Muslims promote. Islam is not a culture but a body of principles and universal values. These universal principles should not be confused with a Pakistani, Turkish or Arabic way of living them. In this way, Islam allows Muslims to adopt aspects of the new cultures and environments in which they find themselves, as long as it does not oppose any clear prohibition specified by their religion.

Thus, while practicing their religion they can preserve certain features of their own culture of origin in the form of richness, not dogma. At the same time they can integrate themselves into European cultures, which becomes a new dimension of their own identity. No one asks that they remain Pakistani or Arabic Muslims but simply Muslims. With time they become Muslims of European culture and build a European Muslim personality shaped through multiple identities: their nationality, their memory, their culture, their religion and their hopes constitute this manifold identity or these integrated multiple identities. This is a process that is not only normal but desirable for them, as well as for their fellow citizens.

Confidence and Creativity

Western Muslims need to find again this intellectual, social and political creativity that has been missing for so long in the Islamic world. Muslims' consciousness here has yet to learn and to formulate in a confident manner an acceptance of European culture through a process of making it their own. They must not keep seeing or perceiving a contradiction between being both Muslim and European, as long as freedom of consciousness and freedom of worship are protected. European legislations recognise and protect the fundamental rights of all citizens and residents. This common legal framework needs to be pushed forward because it allows equality within diversity. Common European citizenship does not prevent a diversity of cultures and of belonging. European societies have been changing and the presence of Muslims has forced it to experience an even greater diversity of cultures. As a result a European identity has evolved that is open, plural and constantly in motion, thanks to the cross-fertilisation between reclaimed cultures of origin and the European culture that now includes its new citizens.

Seen from this perspective, the new European Muslim citizenship enriches the whole society. Muslims should live it and introduce it in this manner to their fellow citizens. Of course, this compels them to come out from the intellectual and social ghettos within which they have lodged themselves, often complacently. Living together and building a truly multicultural society does not mean merely being satisfied with the existence of communities of faith or juxtaposed cultures, whose members ignore each other, never meet and remain enclosed within their own universe of symbolic reference points. Nothing should be stronger in our way of living, and allowing for a mutual exchange of ideas between our communities, than a model of parallel lives, shielded beneath an illusion, which in reality is of mutual ignorance.

Shared Responsibilities

Our responsibilities are shared. Members of the so-called traditional European societies can at times doubt their own identity and are frightened. When this happens they have to refuse any imprisoning reaction by attempting, for example, to draw the boundaries of what they may consider to be an authentic European identity which is 'pure' and uninfected by some 'foreign parasite'. In any period of crisis the temptation to fall back upon phantoms of national identity is stronger than ever as people are carried away by fear, spilling over into the same camp as populists of the extreme right, a phenomenon which we are unfortunately witnessing all over Europe at the moment.

We need to begin by working upon memories. From the Middle Ages, Islam has participated in the building of a European, as well as a British, consciousness in the same way that Judaism or Christianity has. From Shakespeare to Hume, the influences of Islamic civilisation on the literary and philosophical traditions of the time are innumerable. Horizons need to be broadened through the study of these sources, which should be included in the teaching curricula at both secondary and university levels.

This wider, deeper and more subtle understanding of what has moulded European identity throughout history would encourage all people in this society to open up towards each other, including towards Muslims, and to understand that they are not so different or strange when judged by their values and hopes. A truly multicultural society cannot exist without an education in the complexity of what shapes us and in the common dimensions that we share with others, regardless of our differences. The extension of this education consists of developing partnerships willing to engage together in social and political issues that affect us all, including discrimination against women and minorities, racism, unemployment, and other social and urban political issues. European societies must reach this new perception of themselves: of people who are all equal before the law, developing multidimensional identities which are always in motion and flexible enough to defend their shared values. Once again, it remains imperative to distinguish between the social problems and the religious challenges: Muslim and non-Muslim citizens alike need to de-islamise the social fractures for unemployment, violence and marginalisation which have nothing to do with Islam or the Islamic belonging. In this way, the multicultural society of today and tomorrow should succeed in marrying the three dimensions of common citizenship, cultural diversity and a convergence of values within a constantly enriching dynamic of debates, encounters and collective engagement.

This is not an easy task since no one opens up to another person without an effort. It is a matter of studying, reshifting one's focus, shedding one's intellectual and cultural habits and accepting questions from fellow citizens who are not all the same but whose diversity is nonetheless enriching. All the laws in the world will never make us dignified and fair citizens unless we understand that from now on our responsibilities are shared. The law can bring people together and protect them but it cannot manage an identity crisis. This can only be achieved through education, by looking outside and taking the risk of opening up to other cultures, ideas and values, all of which are part of the difficult but exciting challenge of our time.

A Contribution, a new 'We'

There is a contribution that Muslim Europeans and Westerners can bring to their respective societies: reconciliation. Confident in their convictions, frank and rigorous in their critical outlook, armed with a broader understanding of Western societies, of their values, their history and their aspirations, Muslims are ideally placed to engage their fellow citizens in reconciling these societies with their own. The vital issue today is not to compare social models or experiences in a fruitless debate but instead we should take the measure of each society in a far stricter and more demanding way by comparing the ideals affirmed and proclaimed by its intellectuals and politicians with the concrete practices at the social grassroots: human rights and equality of opportunity between men and women, people of different origins and skin colours. We must bring constructive criticism to bear on our societies and measure words against deeds: all citizens must adopt the same healthy self-critical attitude toward their society that Muslims demonstrate towards theirs.

Our societies are awaiting the emergence of a new 'We'. A 'We' that would bring together men and women, citizens of all religion and those without religion who would resolve the contradictions of their society and assert the right to work, to housing, to respect, to stand against racism and all forms of discrimination and offences against human dignity. This 'We' would represent this coming together of citizens confident in their values, defenders of pluralism in their common society and respectful of the identities of others. These citizens would take up the challenge in the name of the shared values at the heart of their societies. As loyal and critical citizens, as men and women of integrity, they will join forces in a revolution of trust and confidence to stem the onrush of fear. Against shallow, emotional, even hysterical reactions they stand firm for rationality, for dialogue, for attentiveness, for a reasonable approach to complex social questions.

Local Initiatives

The future of Western societies is now being played out at the local level. It is a matter of the greatest urgency to set in motion national movements of local initiatives, in which women and men of different religions, cultures and sensitivities can open new horizons of mutual understanding and shared commitment: horizons of trust. These shared projects will bring us together, and give birth to a new 'We' which is anchored in citizenship. Of course, 'intercultural' and 'interfaith' dialogues are both vital and necessary, but they cannot have the impact of the shared commitment of citizens in the priority fields: education, social fractures, insecurity, racism and discrimination, etc.

Together they must learn to question educational programmes, and to propose more inclusive approaches to the sum of remembered experience that make up today's European societies. These societies have changed, and the teaching of history must change also; it must include the multiplicity of these experiences; it must even speak of the dark periods of history, those of which new citizens of the West have often been the original victims. Alongside the Enlightenment and the progress and achievements of science and technology, slavery must be included, colonialism, racism and genocide must be explained objectively, without arrogance or a permanent sense of guilt. A more objective reading of the memories building the current national history must be made official. On the social level we must commit ourselves to a far more thoroughgoing social mixing in our schools and our communities. Far more courageous and creative social and urban policies are needed. But even now citizens can foster human interchange in and through projects focused on local democratic participation. National political authorities must facilitate and encourage such local dynamics.

The Future: a Revolution of Trust

European societies will not win the battle against social insecurity, violence and drugs through a security-based approach alone. What we need in our communities are social institutions, civic education, local job creation, and confidence-building policies. Local political authorities can do much to transform the prevailing atmosphere of suspicion and citizens, including Muslims, must not hesitate to knock on their doors, to remind them that in a democratic society the elected representative is at the service of the voter and not the opposite. It is imperative that we become involved in national affairs, that we do not allow ourselves to be carried away by the passions generated on the international scene. It is clear that a critical discussion of how immigration is managed has yet to take place in Europe: it is no longer possible to strip the Third World of its riches and at the same time treat people who flee poverty and dictatorial regimes as if they were criminals. This is not merely unjust and inhumane; it is intolerable. To be and to remain the voice of the voiceless of Iraq or Palestine, of Tibet or Chechnya, of abused women and of AIDS victims is to take a stand for reconciliation in the name of the ideals of dignity, human rights and justice which are too often sacrificed on the altar of short-term political gain and geostrategic interests. In times of globalisation, both local mutual trust and global critical minds pave the road towards re-conciliation between civilisations.

A revolution of trust and confidence, of critical loyalty, the birth of a new 'We' driven by national movements of local initiatives: such are the contours of a responsible commitment by all the citizens in European societies-for they lay claim to the benefits of a responsible, citizen-based ethic; for they want to promote the Western cultural richness; for they know that survival will de-pend, imperatively, upon a new sense of political creativity. Citizens must work in the long term, above and beyond the electoral deadlines that paralyse politicians and hinder the formulation of innovative, courageous policies. When the elected official has nowhere to turn, when he no longer can trans-late his ideas into reality, it falls to the voters, to the citizens, to lay full claim to their ideals, and to make them a reality.

3

New developments for the welfare of migrants in Europe

Mark RD Johnson

A politics of diversity is emerging in Europe. States increasingly recognise that even if they had previously been exporters of migrants, or transit countries, they have become attractive locations for migrant settlers. Despite many differences between states in their organisation of health care and their experiences of migrants and their origins, there is surprising consistency in the findings of research into the health care needs of migrants and minority ethnic groups across Europe. Expert recommendations were made at a European workshop sponsored by the Portuguese presidency of the European Union in 2007, demonstrating how Portugal, once a net exporter of migrant workers, has now recognised that it now has a significant immigrant population (Dias *et al*, 2005; Fernandes and Pereira, 2008). Recommendations from the workshop in 2007 were expected to be debated by the Council of Ministers. There is a growing degree of international convergence in policy and a common interest among people of migrant origin in the success of these initiatives.

Migrants in Europe

One of the founding principles and most significant effects of the creation of the European Union or 'community' has been the emergence of a free-travel zone for both goods and labour. Essentially, a sort of European citizenship has been created across most of Europe, with freedom of movement not just for travel, but also in many cases to settle. While this is confined to citizens of member states, and may be notionally restricted to those seeking work or who are on holiday, the continuing expansion of the Union has enlarged both the area covered and the populations given these rights.

In advance of accession to the Union, transitional rights have also been granted to many workers who have anticipated the rights they will acquire once their countries of origin are full members of the Union. There are also 'candidate' countries and associate members of the community who have some additional rights or easier access to the travel area, although some states have not fully signed up to the Schengen treaty and retain additional entry controls which may restrict migration into and, in theory, out of their territory. Within those states, however, the rights of admitted workers and their families are much the same as for any other European citizen.

In addition, and attracted by the economic benefits and health of the European Economic Community and the strength of its economy and currency, there are large numbers of 'third country' migrants that is, those coming from states outside the EU. These also can be subdivided into various categories, which have distinctive levels of rights. Legal economic migrants may be restricted by visa requirements but may also have the right to bring members of their family with them and to enjoy the insurance benefits of other employees such as health care/sickness and child benefits and even income guarantees.

Another large and legally defined group is asylum seekers and refugees. There is considerable confusion in popular debate about these groups since refugees who have been granted asylum refugee status should, by law, have equal rights to work and services alongside national citizens under the Geneva Conventions of 1951.

Those seeking asylum may have restrictions placed on their entitlement (Johnson, 2003; Northern Refugee Centre, 2008). On being refused admission or recognition, these rights are normally lost, although national laws may protect them or grant specific rights such as to health care. There are a number of other types of status, such as 'exceptional leave to remain' or 'temporary protection', with variable rights. However, many who have been refused legal status join the ranks of an unquantifiable population of 'undocumented' or illegal migrants. An increasingly large migrant-descended population which may include a number of groups of quite distinctive cultural backgrounds is now developing in every European nation state.

Overall, it is estimated that in 2004-5 there were 25 million non-nationals living in the European Union – including 18 million people who moved into the area from outside the European community (Lavenex, 2007). This means that at least 7 million people took advantage of the freedom of movement to live in another European state than their own. This is a considerable under-estimation of the number of migrants since it takes no account of people moving within their own state or of subsequent immigration or expansion of the EU's borders. However, while these 25 million foreigners make up more than one in twenty of the EU population, they are not evenly spread. Contrary to popular discourse, Britain is not the largest recipient of immigrants: that honour belongs to Latvia, since 20.7 per cent of its population have non-Latvian nationality. Several other countries also have larger populations of migrant origin, including Germany (6.3%), Austria (7.1%), Spain (6.2%) and Cyprus (5.5%), while the UK's foreign-born population represents a mere 3.3 per cent of the total. Nor is the asylum-seeking population a major component of this, although it may have specific and particularly adverse health needs: of the 25 million, only 1.5 are refugees and half of that total are located in Germany. According to the UK HM Treasury in 2006, migrants were worth a net £6bn to the national economy. This is rarely alluded to in political debates, or in any discussion about the rights and needs of migrants but 'the main debate on the integration of migrants has focused on other issues than health' (Padilla and Miguel, 2007) and has been predominantly adverse.

In policy terms, there is some concern to develop a set of agreed terms for use in defining migrants and other 'Groups of Interest' for social policy reasons such as ensuring public health and supporting community cohesion. Not all of these terms are equally acceptable or appropriate for use across Europe, and some states actively prohibit the recording of data using one or other of these dimensions (Makkonen, 2007; Johnson, 2008; Johnson and Borde, 2009). Key themes include Race/Ethnicity used in Britain and the US, Language/Religion/Culture (variably collected and highly specific to different areas of social policy and nations), Citizenship/ Nationality (which is widely used as a definition in much of mainland Europe, along with 'birthplace' origin, while terms such as Black and Minority Ethnic are largely confined to British use.

Similarly, the definition of Asylum-Seeker/Refugee may vary or be differently understood in popular and official usage, and is seldom if ever recorded in service use monitoring data. Meanwhile Roma, Traveller and Gypsy populations exist in most European countries but are equally invisible to statistics or are not regarded in some states as being 'migrant' populations despite the fact that they are not settled but move without having permanent addresses and can be shown to have worse health than the majority populations. A final category, not really recognised in Britain although possibly increasing in significance as devolution gives additional rights or distinctiveness to Scottish, Welsh and Northern Irish people is that of national minorities who may have specific rights or distinctive languages and cultural traditions such as the Breton or Occitan speakers of France and the Sud-Tirolean population of northern Italy.

Political and Legislative Drivers

Although there is well established data (Carballo *et al*, 1997) and anecdotal or politically informed evidence that testifies to the health inequalities affecting populations of migrant and minority origin across Europe, there is evidence of a change in policy and practice to address and counter these disadvantages. These can be seen to be driven by a number of forces, including both moral and pragmatic arguments as well as by the force of legislation and protocol. These latter have been encapsulated in the European and Universal Conventions on Human Rights and more recently were addressed, updated and extended in the EU Treaty of Amsterdam 1997 (www.eurotreaties.com/amsterdamtreaty.pdf) encoded in particular in Article 13 and subsequent regulations and schemes required by the treaty of all member states.

Thus discrimination on the grounds of 'sex, racial or ethnic origin, religion or belief, disability, age or sexual orientation' is starting to be outlawed, although it is clearly still practised both on a personal and institutional level in many places and is not fully addressed in many others. In relation to health, we can see that the high moral principles of the World Health Organisation's 1978 Alma Ata declaration of intent: 'Health for All' subsequently amended to 'by the year 2000' have been at least partially effective in driving change (www.righttohealthcare.org/Docs/DocumentsC.htm).

On a more pragmatic level, there is recognition that health and related care form a part of the 'The Social Wage' or, in older Marxist terms, the 'indirect costs of reproduction of labour', and that there is a degree of self-interest not only among capitalists, employers and investors, and across society, in guaranteeing the health and social welfare of those who travel to fill key roles in the manufacturing, service and support economies of the west. It is really a form of pure enlightened self interest that migrant and minority workers, who are more likely to fill the least desirable jobs and work for the lowest rates of pay, should have any necessary medical care provided through the subsidised route of public health care. Otherwise either their wages will have to rise, or the jobs may not be done or more migrants will be required to cover their time off work, which would be equally unpalatable to the political groups who oppose anything that encourages migrants!

Deeply embedded in our society, there is a moral argument that suggests that the community should support its weakest members and assist the deserving poor and those who need help: 'From each according to their ability; to each according to their need'. This was attributed to Karl Marx, but also derives from the Christian New Testament (Acts of the Apostles, Chapter 2, v44-45). This was embodied in a recent debate in the Council of Europe, which many regard as the main protagonist for human rights in Europe, and whose debates and papers inform much of the human rights agenda of the European Community as well. The main recommendations of that debate are presented below. They emphasise the rights of migrants to retain their cultural identity and for this to be recognised in their healthcare:

Council of Europe Recommendation 2006-18

The Committee of Ministers recommends that the governments of member states:

i.   consider issues related to the improvement of access and quality of health care services in multicultural societies as one of the priority areas of action in health care policy;

ii. develop coherent and comprehensive policies and strategies addressing health care needs in multicultural societies, including prevention;

iii. promote an intersectoral and multidisciplinary approach to health problems and health care delivery in multicultural societies, taking into consideration the rights of multicultural populations;

iv. promote the involvement and participation of all parties concerned (researchers, policy makers, local health authorities, health professionals, representatives of ethnic minority groups and non-governmental organisations) in the planning, implementation and monitoring of health policies for multicultural populations;

v.   embed health issues of multicultural populations in the legal framework as an integral part of the general health system;

vi. develop a knowledge base on the health of multicultural populations through systematic data collection and research;

vii. promote the inclusion of ethnic minority groups in culturally appropriate/ adapted programmes promoting health and prevention, and in research and quality management;

Recommendation Rec (2006)18 of the Committee of Ministers to member states on health services in a multicultural society (*Adopted by the Committee of Ministers on 8 November 2006 at the 979th meeting of the Ministers' Deputies*) https://wcd.coe.int/ViewDoc.jsp?id=1062769&BackC

There are also pragmatic arguments such as the recognition that the public health is better preserved if migrants are kept healthy (Dodge, 1969) – and that this is not simply restricted to refusing access to unhealthy migrants, since there is substantial evidence that for most migrants, health deteriorates after finding work and becoming employed. This is because of the conditions of work and the exploitation of marginal labour, the migrants' desire to save and repatriate funds, or their ignorance about how to stay healthy in an unfamiliar environment, including how to access health care support or deal with unfamiliar diseases. Early intervention reduces costs of health care and improves productivity in the workforce and there is extensive evidence that migrant workers are more likely to seek treatment later than others and in the case of infectious diseases, they are potentially a reservoir for infections such as tuberculosis or sexually transmitted diseases and other diseases associated with poverty and illegality.

New Policy Drivers and Influences

It must also be recognised that there have been a number of initiatives and moves to highlight the needs of multicultural and migrant populations and to support or share good practice, drawing on the enthusiasm of health workers and academic researchers. Some of these are listed below with internet links to sites where further information can be found. The growing networks of practitioners and researchers are increasing the body of research-based knowledge to support evidence-based policy and practice and at the same time creating a professional and pragmatic consensus about the value of such adaptations to health care services, including information on its cost-effectiveness and the need to obtain political support and governmental action. These are supported by the efforts of migrant workers and associations of social/cultural or moral agencies such as councils of faiths and groups such as the South Asian Health Foundation (UK), which is largely formed of medical professionals whose own or whose parents' roots lie on the Indian subcontinent. They believe that they have a duty to support research and campaigning for the health of their ethnic group (www.sahf.org.uk).

A workshop hosted by the Portuguese Ministry of Health during the period of the Portuguese Presidency of the European Community was at least in part the product of the activity of such groups, allied with academics and policy researchers. At this event, a series of speakers reported on policy and practice in a selection of states and a consensus statement was approved which was passed to the European commission to inform future directives and policy development. Through all of these activities a growing database of evidence and consensus on ways forward is developing so that the idea of improving the health conditions of migrant populations is no longer seen as strange or unachievable. This may be supported by market-led pressures such as suggestions by medical insurance companies that failure to take account of the needs of migrant people's specific needs, including language support – may increase costs and prove to be an insurance risk (Haslam, 2008). In such ways, as well as the growing economic and political strength of migrants, change is brought about.

Migrant Friendly Hospitals: A European project sponsored by the European Commission, DG Health and Consumer Protection (SANCO) brought together hospitals from 12 member states of the European Union, experts, international organisations and networks. These partners agreed to put migrant-friendly, culturally competent health care and health promotion higher on the European health policy agenda and to support other hospitals by compiling practical knowledge and instruments to improve practice.

http://www.mfh-eu.net/public/european_recommendations.htm

The Task Force on Migrant Friendly Hospitals was subsequently established in the framework of the WHO Network on Health Promoting Hospitals to carry on the work of the original EU working group: http://www.hph-hc.cc/projects.php#mfh

EU-COST Action 'HOME' – an EU European Science Foundation-supported programme of working groups to consolidate and review work carried out so far, recommend ways forward and stimulate scientific and technical co-operation around migrant health including with social and policy factors, migrants' state of health, and improvements in service delivery.

http://www.cost.esf.org/index.php?id=233&action_number=IS0603

MigHealthNet: The MIGHEALTHNET project aims to stimulate the exchange of knowledge on migrant and minority health through the development of interactive data bases in each of the participating countries (Organised as 'wikis' on the principle of Wikipedia): http://www.mighealth.net/index.php/Main_Page

International Centre for Migration and Health, a WHO Collaborating Centre to develop a consensus on international training for cultural competence in healthcare, based in Geneva Switzerland: www.ICMH.CH

South Asian Health Foundation: an association largely led by doctors in Britain who are of Indian, Pakistani or Bangladeshi ethnic origin, campaigning for research and development in addressing the specific health care needs of South Asian communities in the UK. www.sahf.org.uk

---

A History of Migrations

While it might appear that the current phase of political and policy interest in migrant health is unique, there has been a long-standing interest and concern about migration and its impact on public health. As long ago as 1905, in the first Aliens Act passed in Britain, concern was expressed about the migration of people of Jewish origin and other European 'refugees' to Britain and the risk they might pose to the public health. Similar concerns have recurred every time major population movements have taken place, including during the Second World War (1939-45), which led to movements of displaced persons in the 1940s. Their homes and livelihoods had been destroyed during the war, some were forced to move by occupying powers and subsequently by the movement of 'European Volunteer Workers' (EVWs).

This was when the Geneva Conventions on the rights of refugees were drawn up, on whose principles many migrants and states still rely. During the 1960s many European states, notably France, the Netherlands and Britain, became the destination of migrants from their former colonies or overseas territories, as these gained independence and because the economy of the 'home' (ie European) country needed the additional labour power to fuel its economic expansion. At first the majority of migrants were single men, who had few health problems except for industrial accidents, alcohol use and sexually transmitted diseases. In the 1970s there was a process of Family Reunification when wives and children came to join the men, creating a more complete and stable society but presenting new challenges to health care, in particular child health, antenatal care and perinatal mortality, immunisation and childhood diseases of poverty such as rickets (Vitamin D deficiency) (Samanta *et al*, 2009). Some of these issues have continued to recur in new migrant groups to this day where we are seeing a resurgence of olsteomalacia or rickets.

Since the 1980s Europe has been the destination of many waves of refugees and asylum seekers affected by world-wide conflicts, environmental disasters, political instability and the economic destitution associated with this. There are also significant numbers of so-called 'irregular migrants' who may be trafficked or assisted to migrate to seek a better life or to meet the demands of economic forces. Some of these are illegal or marginal, such as the demand for prostitutes and domestic servants in more advantaged economies. The whole notion of the European Community as a 'single travel area' or 'European economic community' is founded on the concept of the free movement of labour as well as trade to facilitate economic activity. The continued expansion of the EU from its origins in the European Steel and Coal Community, from seven to the present membership and a waiting list including Turkey and other 'candidate states', especially the accession of A8 states in 2006, has created large population movements and demands on healthcare provision, including the need for information in languages not previously spoken in the host nations.

Some Consensus Statements

From the research and conferences of these networks, a number of common threads and agreements emerge. These include recognition that, despite the popular images promoted by certain political groups and tabloid newspapers, migrants and migrant descended populations are not overall consumers of welfare. They actually generate health care services and welfare support for themselves. They also make it possible, through their role as workers in the caring services, to maintain the levels of healthcare which the majority host populations of the richer states are accustomed to. Migrants and migrant descended populations actively create welfare through enlarging the number of voluntary sector organisations, and the fact that many cultures see caring for strangers as normal behaviour: in more deprived areas community-based agencies support not only members of the minority community but also poorer members of the host society. The Board of Deputies of British Jews and the J-CORE organisation (www.jcore.org.uk) have documented how earlier migrations of European Jews created an active and economically powerful network of support services in Britain.

As suggested earlier, migrants generally come to the EU healthy and lose their relative health advantage after living and working here for a time. This has yet to be fully explained by research: it is possible that the migration process is stressful and expensive for people who are not intrinsically healthy. Subsequent discrimination and stress arising from racial or political tension may reduce their ability to fight off ill-health, and so might the risks inherent in lower-paid and marginal occupations. Social exclusion is well known to be a health hazard, and 'newness' may also be a risk factor, in the shape of difficulty in accessing information, unfamiliarity with the symptoms of diseases more common and curable in Europe, and the failure to understand how the health service works and the availability of preventive care such as immunisation and screening. There is also the hazard of poverty: it remains true that services may be inappropriate or provided in inaccessible ways at times or in places that are difficult for migrant workers and their families. They may also be afraid of authority and avoid situations where documents may be required.

Health care workers and health care services are also poorly designed to meet the needs of migrant and minority ethnic people. There are ethnic differences in patterns of disease, including greater susceptibility to certain types of illness. Such issues are notably diabetes associated worldwide with migration, or cultural variations in the presentation of symptoms of illness and culturally specific perceptions of health, body and disease: this may create problems for people in describing their health needs or understanding the explanations and advice they are given. Some, but not all, of these are linguistic and may be overcome by the use of language support services such as interpreters but others are more deep-rooted.

People's previous encounters with services may inform not only their future behaviour but also that of their families, friends and social networks, especially if they are the first of their community to seek help and they are disappointed, rebuffed or feel discriminated against. The perceived or real effects of racism can be a genuine health hazard both to the individual and to public health. Even if unintended, this includes the impact of cultural or religious ignorance and failure to appreciate ethnically specific aspects of diseases and treatment relating to migrant minority populations.

It may be that some migrants do not use existing services and might even avoid them and health surveillance systems designed to ensure better public health generally, and instead choose alternative treatment options. These include access to healthcare using traditional medical practices such as Chinese herbal medicine, or unani and ayurvedic *hakims* or *Vaids* in the Indian tradition. There is little evidence that this prevents minorities from accessing the normal allopathic or western medical services which are known to cure common diseases, but they will probably use traditional treatments for long-term or chronic conditions or those for which there is no traditional cultural explanation such as 'evil eye' or witchcraft, and when western medicines do not produce immediate results. It is also increasingly the case that migrants and their descendants may return to their ancestral homelands if this means that they can get quicker or cheaper treatment with the added bonus of being able to visit friends and religious or cultural sites. This is quite usual for people of Indian origin, since the Indian medical establishment is largely familiar with western medical technology, English-speaking, often trained in UK hospitals, and eager to develop private practice earning foreign currency.

Conclusion

Finally, we should consider the recommendations of the EU workshop in Lisbon. These are as follows:

The Lisbon Recommendations

Migrants are an important resource for Europe and the EU needs them. They contribute to demographic and economic growth. The healthier they are the easiest the intercultural dialogue, more feasible the integration and the larger their contribution to economic growth.

Coherent immigration policies which incorporate a proper consideration of the health dimension are essential at both EU and Member State level. Health should also be considered a key component of integration and cooperation for development with the countries of origin. Moreover, health should be included in the EU Charter of Migrants' Rights.

The forthcoming European Health Strategy and the Health Services Framework should address migrant health issues.

Employment and social policies should consider health needs of migrant workers as well as the gender aspects of migration and health. In this sense it is important to ratify and implement the UN and ILO conventions on migrant workers.

Non communicable diseases, as cardiovascular diseases and diabetes, also largely affect migrants. They require specific approaches, as those aiming at the whole populations, but also at the high risk individuals.

Due to the particular circumstances of migration and settlement, migrants may be particularly vulnerable to mental health problems. Special emphasis should be set on entitlement and accessibility to mental health services, on the promotion of high-quality and culturally sensitive mental health care and on encouraging migrants to actively participate in the provision of services and the definition of their own needs.

Migrant women and children, who are among the most vulnerable of the migrant populations, should be considered a priority and targeted if necessary through outreach programmes. Specific actions should include access to family planning services and education, sexual and reproductive health, guarantee vaccination and immunisation programmes, and prevention of domestic violence and human trafficking.

Global problems call for global answers; health and migration are global phenomena that call for urgent global responses. As migration transcends national borders and is a global issue, the EU should assume a leading role in this global challenge. What is more, health is a major element of human rights. Migrants and their descendants should have access to health care as a way to promote the integration and the well-being of the whole population, if necessary adopting positive discrimination practices. There is increasingly, at least in higher policy circles in Europe, some sign of movement to adopt and promote this attitude and to develop better practices to preserve and support the health of migrants. These will, hopefully, also benefit the populations of minority ethnic origin, descendants of migrants in Britain and elsewhere in Europe and prevent newer generations of migrant origin, including new migrant flows, from having to repeat the experiences of previous 'waves' in overcoming resistance, exclusion and poverty to obtain basic human rights.

References

Carballo, M, Divino, JJ and Zeric, D (1997) *Analytic review of Migration and health and as it affects European Community Countries – report to EC* (Project SOC 201600 05F01) Geneva: International Centre for Migration and Health

Dias, B, Farinha T, Freitas I, Ribiero M, Rosario E, Seabra H and Silva E (2005) *The Situation of Immigrants and Ethnic Minorities in Portugal in 2005 – Annual Report for the European Monitoring Centre on Racism and Xenophobia.* Numena:Centro de investigacao en ciancias socials, Lisbon, Portugal www.numena.org.pt/ficheiros/RAXEN%20Annual%20Report%202005.pdf
Date accessed May 2009

Dodge, JS (1969) *The Fieldworker in Immigrant Health.* London: Staples Press

Fernandes, A, Pereira MJ (Eds.) (2008) *Saude e Migracoes na UE (Health and Migration in the EU: Better health for all in an inclusive society)* Lisbon: National Institute of Health, Ministry of Health Portugal for the European Commission (www.insa.pt) Conference proceedings

Haslam, J, (2008) Practice Finance: How to ... Meet the needs of non-English speakers. *GP Magazine* April 30th (www.healthcarerepublic.com)

Johnson, MRD (2003) *Asylum seekers in dispersal – healthcare issues.* Home Office Online Report 13/03 www.homeoffice.gov.uk/rds/pdfs2/rdsolr1303.pdf May 2009

Johnson MRD (2008) Making Difference Count: Ethnic Monitoring in Health (and Social Care) *Radical Statistics* # 96 :38-45 (Equity and Accountability in the NHS)(Ed.) S Ruane, 2008

Johnson, MRD and Borde, T (2009) 'Representation of ethnic minorities in research – Necessity, opportunity and adverse effects' in (Eds Lorraine Culley, Nicky Hudson and Floor van Rooij) *Marginalized Reproduction: Ethnicity, Infertility and Reproductive Technologies.* London: Earthscan Chapter 4 :64-80

Lavenex, S (2007) *Focus-Migration: European Union Hamburg: Netzwerk Migration in Europa.* http://www.focus-migration.de/European_Union.6003.0.html?&L=1 (accessed 6 May 2009)

Makkonen, T (2007) European handbook on equality data. Brussels: European Commission Directorate-General for Employment, Social Affairs and Equal Opportunities http://ec.europa.eu/employment_social/fundamental_rights/pdf/pubst/stud/hb07_en.pdf accessed May 2009

Northern Refugee Centre (2008) *Entitlements to health care for persons from abroad* (Updated posting March 5th 2008) http://www.nrcentre.org.uk/index.php?option=com_content&view=article&id=98:entitlements-to-health-care-for-persons-from-abroad&catid=23:entitlement-to-health-care&Itemid=57 (accessed 6 May 2009)

Padilla, B, and Pereira Miguel, J (2007) *Health and Migration in the EU: Building a Shared Vision for Action,* http://www.eu2007.min-saude.pt/NR/rdonlyres/9D113E93-736E-4F5E-BC6BD66781 BA8CBA/7677/Visiondoc.pdf

Samanta, A, Johnson, MRD, Guo F and Adebajo A (2009) Snails in bottles and language cuckoos: an evaluation of patient information resources for South Asians with osteomalacia (*Rheumatology,* doi: 10.1093/rheumatology/ken464)

4

Sickle Cell:
a signifier for the New Europe

Simon Dyson

Introduction

Amulti-ethnic New Europe presents a challenge in the form of a paradox. Whilst we might celebrate difference, we know that for some people difference is constructed as a challenge of the *Other*, who is automatically to be distrusted for that alleged difference. And yet if we emphasise our similarities, this means that we create the discursive space in which uniformity in the provision of health, education and welfare services can (wrongly) be justified. This uniformity in the face of diversity lacks cultural competence, and ultimately fails the diversity within ethnic majorities as well as ethnic minorities themselves (Gunaratnam, 2001). What we lack is a model that signifies, at one and the same time, our connectedness *and* our difference.

The chapter starts with a brief outline of sickle cell and why it simultaneously signifies both difference and connectedness in terms of genes and bodies, and bodies and geographical place. It then moves on to discuss the model that sickle cell provides in connection with key issues at the heart of European social policy. These issues include the experiences of asylum seekers and refugees, immigration, access to health and welfare services, criminal justice and security, and community cohesion. For each of these social policy issues, the challenges, changing experiences and in some cases resolutions suggested by the case of sickle cell are discussed.

The significance of sickle cell

Sickle cell disorders are serious genetic chronic illnesses which can affect many systems of the body and produce a wide range of debilitating symptoms including episodes of extreme pain, anaemia, jaundice, acute chest problems, strokes and vulnerability to infection. Sickle cell is of particular relevance to many established and recently migrated minority ethnic groups across Europe. The World Health Organisation (1988) noted over twenty years ago that a rise in sickle cell was likely in countries such as the UK, France, the Netherlands and Portugal because of migration associated with the former colonies of these countries in Africa and the Caribbean. More recently, Gulbis *et al* (2006) have recorded the predominantly Congolese and Moroccan ancestry of people with sickle cell in Belgium. However, contrary to popular wisdom, sickle cell does not automatically mean African ancestry. Whilst four of the known variations of the gene associated with sickle cell arose in Africa, a fifth variation originated in Arabia and India (Serjeant and Serjeant, 2001). Furthermore, one of the African variations, the Benin type, occurs extensively around the Mediterranean and was found there in the eighth century (Lavinha *et al*, 1992), hence the occasional presence of sickle cell and related genes in people with white skin, blonde hair or blue eyes (Lehmann and Huntsman, 1974).

Stuart Hall described the concept of race as a 'floating signifier' (Hall, 1997), meaning that there is no essential meaning of the concept of race: it always derives its meaning contextually, in terms of its relation to other signs in systems of meaning. Sickle cell has been described both as an 'emblematically black' issue (Hall, 2003:6), and as one of the negative signifiers of race (Chambers, 2003:21-39), that is the black body is somehow essentially different from other bodies.

Yet in social policy we seem not to know what to do with the concept of race. The American Anthropological Association (1998) rejects it for much the same reason that the 1950 UNESCO statement did so: there are no distinct biological races. In contrast, the American Sociological Association (2003) insists on the retention of this concept, in order to remain connected to the ideas people use in everyday life. However, whilst it is legitimate to study the way in which people use race as if it had a biological reality in constructing their lives, either to discriminate against or to advance black politics, this is not the same as studying race (Carter, 2007). One unintended consequence of the view that political blackness represents the best strategy for advancement is that it permits the continued elision of race as a political strategy and race as a biologically-grounded identity, and renders the anchoring of negative meanings to that term more possible.

Sickle cell would usually be evoked as a negative signifier and serve a conservative political project that is distrustful of immigration, wary of perceived over-consumption of welfare services, and in extremes, violently hostile to Black people. However, a scientific understanding of sickle cell as an issue disrupts the presumed relationship between sign and signified. Thus whilst sickle cell signifies challenges, it also signals the possible policy initiatives needed, across many of the domains of contemporary European social policy.

Asylum seekers and refugees

Asylum seekers and refugees may only discover the full implications of the fact that they or their children have genes associated with sickle cell once they come to Europe and have their blood screened in a laboratory as part of ante-natal or neonatal care. The civil unrest in Sierra Leone brought one family with two children with sickle cell to London in 1997. The mother recounts how they were unprepared for the northern European winter; how the symptoms of sickle cell changed in a new country, because of weather (Jones *et al*, 2005); air pollution (Yallop *et al*, 2007); or the experience of racism (Anionwu and Atkin, 2001), and how treatments also differed:

> We arrived in the UK in December wearing our traditional African clothes. A month after our arrival Kenneth had his first sickle-cell crisis: abdominal pain and speech difficulties. He was admitted to Guy's Hospital for a week. It was during this time that I at last began to understand more about the disease; I became aware of new treatments, such as phenoxymethylpenicillin, and of other related problems, such as respiratory infection. In fact, pulmonary infections became a recurring problem for Kenneth soon after we moved to the UK (Buckner, 2004:1361).

A number will also be caught up in the politics of seeking asylum. The case of Frank Kiore from Burundi is one such instance:

> My name is Frank Kiore. I am 21 years old and an asylum seeker from Burundi. I also have Sickle Cell Anaemia. I left my parents in Burundi four years ago due to the war that is still going on in Burundi. I am here in the UK because I need medical attention that I wasn't able to get back in Burundi, so I can get on with my life. (NCADC, 2005)

In other cases the issue has centred on the breaking of family ties. One seventeen year old with sickle cell anaemia, Kwaku Acheampong, had an entitlement to stay in the UK, but his mother was deported back to Ghana by private jet when she became so distressed at having to leave her sick son that other airlines refused to transport her (BBC News, 2000). In a further case, a woman from the Democratic Republic of the Congo was carrying twins as a consequence of being raped:

> P is a 20 year old Rwandan failed asylum-seeker from DRC who is six months pregnant with twins. She left after the murder of her family and her own rape. She has recently made a fresh asylum/human rights claim. She sleeps in her bed with scissors at night because she is afraid she may be attacked. She needs extra ante-natal care and tests because sickle cell trait has been found and because of her mental ill-health and the extra needs of twins. She has not been able to attend hospital appointments or GP appointments because she cannot walk the several miles and has no cash. It is now too late in her pregnancy to carry out sickle cell tests in relation to the embryos. (Housing and Immigration Group, 2006)

The challenge for service provision within a diverse Europe is that in the UK, for example, the main post-1945 migration of those of African descent was associated with people of African-Caribbean descent, and less so those of recent African descent. It is important to note the West and Central African origins of our examples. The relevance is that one in ten of the British African-Caribbean population are sickle cell carriers and 0.2 per cent will have a sickle cell disorder. By contrast, those of West and Central African descent may have carrier rates close to one in four, with 2 per cent having a sickle cell disorder. Planning of services on the basis of an undifferentiated 'black' population is therefore inadequate. Dyson *et al* (2007) show how a relatively small change in the African population of one city can lead to a sizeable increase in the numbers of sickle cell carriers identified at clinics who require different screening policies than those previously adopted by commissioners.

Immigration

The issue of sickle cell is highly pertinent to a number of people resisting deportation by the immigration authorities. The implications of sickle cell for migrants to European countries include:

- whether health care for their chronic illness can be secured at all;
- the health perils of immigration detention and/ return travel to country of origin,
- environmental health threats and quality of care for their complex illness in their country of origin.

One such example includes a migrant to Eire facing multiple challenges:

> The government is currently trying to deport Grace Efe Afekhai, a Nigerian woman, and her son. Grace has since been getting cancer treatment in the Mater Hospital in Dublin. Her son has been diagnosed with sickle cell anaemia, which needs constant monitoring and treatment. With proper care, people with sickle cell live into their forties, but in Nigeria, Daniel would be unlikely to live beyond the age of 20. (Residents Against Racism, Ireland, 2005)

There are several justifiable reasons why children with sickle cell disorder might be more vulnerable upon return to their home country in Africa. First, the infant would be vulnerable to early death in childhood from infection (Ohene-Frempong and Nkrumah, 1994). Second, much of sub-Saharan Africa is malarial, and, contrary to popular belief, people with sickle cell disorders are more vulnerable to death from malaria than others. Third, much of Africa relies on fee-for-service payments for health and the perception that children with sickle cell will cost families money is one of the reasons behind the widespread stigmatisation of those with sickle cell disorders in Africa (Dennis-Antwi, 2006). Thus the fear of increased levels of illness, raised risk of premature death, additional stresses of societal discrimination and relative lack of affordable services are well-founded.

These issues are at the heart of contestation in immigration matters and are increasing. The increasing number of cases include Abdulrahim Abimbola, a two year old with sickle cell anaemia from Nigeria who is especially susceptible to malaria having had no environmental exposure to malaria as well as the extra vulnerability of having sickle cell anaemia (NCADC, 2002); Emmanuel Laolu-Balogun, a fourteen year old Nigerian with sickle cell anaemia, whose short notice of deportation would not have permitted the time for the required weeks of anti-malarial tablets to be taken (NCADC, 2008); Olivier Mmounda à Nyam, a 28 year old asylum seeker from Cameroon, fearing return to Cameroon for speaking out against the government's treatment of people with sickle cell, who, once threatened with deportation, underwent several sickle cell crises and one suicide attempt (*Independent Media Centre UK*, 2008).

Moreover, in the processes of appeals for leave to remain in the UK, those living with a sickle cell disorder are vulnerable to detention, even if this contravenes the Immigration and Nationality Directorate's policy on the unsuitability of detainees with a chronic illness for detention. One detainee with a sickle cell disorder reports that he was detained despite a clear statement to the officer that he suffered constant pain with his sickle cell. His account alleges a series of injustices, including:

- failure to arrange a medical examination within 24 hours
- failure of a nurse to respond to the early signs of a sickle cell crisis
- placing him in an extremely cold cell with other detainees who smoked heavily, so precipitating a series of a sickle cell crises
- lack of disabled access restricting the possibility of washing
- the refusal of a doctor to write stating his medical condition
- the refusal of a doctor to allow him access to his medical notes
- the deterioration in his health such that his movements were incapacitated
- the refusal of staff to call an ambulance until forced to do so by the actions of other inmates
- the lack of privacy in any medical consultation, the 'disposal' of all his personal property by staff
- a further refusal to call an ambulance for a sickle cell crisis
- a five hour transfer to another detention centre rather than to hospital for treatment of the crisis
- a disabled person required to climb flights of stairs to obtain medication
- a restriction of pain medication
- refusing access to medical records
- the doctoring of medical notes, only obtained at all through the actions of a sympathetic nurse (Adesina, 2007).

Such a catalogue of inadequate medical treatment reflects the wider inadequate treatment of those living with sickle cell disorders in the custody of the state (Plugge *et al*, 2006: 71).

Health services

Sickle cell originated in areas of the world that were malarial, including much of sub-Saharan Africa as far south as the Zambesi River and parts of Eastern Arabia and India. The sickle cell gene was not found originally within black-skinned populations of Southern Africa, but one of the origins of the gene did occur in lighter-skinned populations of Eastern Arabia and India. This means that the popular association of black skin and sickle cell is misplaced (Serjeant and Serjeant, 2001). As early as 1963, medical commentators were anticipating the changing nature of medical care that would be required in the

UK with a changing population (Lehmann, 1963). Yet 25 years later this had to be emphasised by the World Health Organisation, as if new: it was noted that migration from the former African, Caribbean, Arab and Indian sub-continent colonies of Britain, France, Portugal and the Netherlands to Europe would bring sickle cell to greater prominence as a health issue in countries previously referred to as 'non-endemic' areas for sickle cell (WHO, 1988).

More recently, haematologists who are more used to working with other blood-related disorders such as leukaemia or haemophilia, have referred to 'immigration haematology', to signify the need for these consultants in the UK and France to adapt their practice to the new prevalence of sickle cell in European countries (Roberts and de Montalembert, 2007). This does not ack-nowledge the long-standing British-born communities with sickle cell, nor explain why changing medical practice attendant upon immigration, noted nearly half a century earlier, is still being construed as 'new'.

The development of services for sickle cell in the UK has been excruciatingly slow. Over the years, the provision of health and welfare services has been one of documented neglect (Prashar et al, 1985); a lack of unified health service provision (Franklin, 1990); pressure from the community as the main im-petus for the development of services (Anionwu, 1993); systematic shortages of specialist sickle cell workers in areas of greatest need (Department of Health, 1993); a lack of development of social services (Ahmad and Atkin, 1996), and a marginalisation of sickle cell as a predominantly ethnic rather than a mainstream health issue (Dyson, 2005).

In the UK it was not until the NHS Plan which began to systematise the new-born screening of all children for SCD, that sickle cell made an appearance in formal written government health policy (Department of Health, 2000). By the time England had implemented comprehensive screening of newborn children to identify, and begun early life-saving treatment for infants with sickle cell, sickle cell was already four times as common as phenylketonuria, for which a comparable newborn screening programme had existed for over thirty years.

There has been a similar long time lapse between the identification of sickle cell as an emerging health issue in Europe (Lehmann, 1963) and the docu-mentation of the changing nature of health needs in individual countries across Europe including the UK (Thomas-Hope, 1992); Norway (Graesdal et al, 2001); Italy (Giordano et al, 2005); and the Netherlands (Russo-Mancuso et al, 2003).

Without recognition in formal health policy, the responses of health services throughout Europe may be ill-informed and unresponsive and they may struggle to provide appropriate services. Support groups in Eire and Holland attest to this. In Eire the support group is recent:

> I have just started the sickle cell association in Dublin hoping to help people living with sickle cell like myself. [...] Sickle Cell is not recognised in Ireland and only few people (Doctors, Consultants) understand it in-depth. I am hoping to draw a lot of people with sickle cell living in Ireland together and start a forum where we can help each other as best as we can and probably get the Health Ministry to recognise it as a life threatening disease. (Lawal, 2007)

The support group in the Netherlands is more established, but the words of their president suggest a huge struggle to obtain the best treatment:

> We have had a lot of problems getting the GPs and hospitals to recognise that the sickle cell ... is also a Dutch problem, many of the patients feel that they are discriminated, and that it has taken too long to know whether they were carriers. They feel that their rights have not been addressed; I have two families that want to take this to the European Courts ... we still do not have enough doctors that will check for carriers. The treatment in some areas is very good, in other areas disgraceful; however I know that this is the same in the UK. Many patients, certainly the first generation hate the health service, and have many difficulties in accepting the illness. (Organisation for Sickle Cell Anaemia Research, Netherlands, 2007)

The painfully slow development of service provision associated with sickle cell shows up the broader failure to respond positively to the needs of ethnic minorities in the new Europe of the early twenty first century.

Welfare services

The challenge for the welfare services of a New Europe is to recognise and respond to the changing profile and needs of multiethnic populations. Frequently, this has involved a systematic over-emphasis on presumed difference. Patterns of mortality and morbidity have been wrongly assumed to be different on the basis of genetics or culture. The reliance on mortality data which only records country of birth, and not ethnicity has led to perceptions of differences in health which may be specific to the generation involved in migration and not to subsequent generations. Alleged raised levels of 'Asian' heart disease in the UK are actually an indicator of levels of material deprivation (Nazroo, 1999). Patterns of mental illness, once controlled for the effects of levels of social support and social capital, reflect the differential responses of mental health services as much as any underlying difference in rates of mental distress (Sprotson and Nazroo, 2002).

In the UK, sickle cell has been mobilised to show that health authorities are doing something to promote the health of ethnic minorities, whilst health initiatives relevant to numerically greater causes of premature death, such as heart disease, hypertension and diabetes, were initially ignored (Bhopal and Donaldson, 1988). The problem is that having played a part in a symbolic, rather than actual, response to ethnic minority health needs, sickle cell remained relatively neglected, with its first appearance in statutory, funded UK health policy as late as 2000 (Department of Health, 2000).

With the historic neglect of sickle cell as a health issue, its neglect in wider welfare services is potentially rendered even more stark, since other services can and do dismiss the issues as the responsibility of health services. In the education system, children with sickle cell are faced with challenges, not so much from their sickle cell as much as from lack of supportive school policies. Schools are not implementing policies on helping young people with sickle cell to catch up lessons missed or to implement simple preventive measures to stop them becoming ill in the first place. There is no recognition of the need to be proactive in challenging racialising and disabling discourses that surround the young person living with sickle cell (Dyson *et al*, 2009). Youth and community work is associated with interventions around young people's rights and perspectives; mediating with bureaucracies, providing innovative frames for youth activity, and certain specific initiatives around such issues as drugs education.

The contested site of treatment for severe painful sickle cell crises with opiate-based drugs leads to young black patients being stereotyped by health workers as recreational drug users (Anionwu and Atkin, 2001). Treatment for sickle cell reflects a medical division of labour between paediatric and adult services: services suitable for 13-25 year olds, in common with services for young people of that age with sickle cell or other chronic illnesses, are currently lacking (Yates *et al*, 2009).

The housing needs of those with sickle cell – to be warm, free from infection-inducing damp; free of stress in terms of residential location; and for those with mobility needs not in high-rise flats – are inversely related to the likely allocation of housing to ethnic minority groups.

Thus sickle cell generates challenges not only for health services but for education, youth work and housing services too. Those local authorities who are likely to respond best in the provision of welfare services relevant to sickle cell are those who are prepared to see the issues of service provision in complex terms rather than within a single policy framework.

Criminal justice, security and terrorism

Beckett (1999) has suggested that an unexpected death in custody represents an important point of public scrutiny within the criminal justice system, especially when the victim is from an ethnic minority community. Alton Manning's death under restraint by prison guards was one of several sudden deaths of black men in custody in the UK during the 1990s. The Director of the UK Prison Service was pressed to explain why there had been a spate of sudden deaths of black men in custody. He is quoted as saying that 'Afro-Caribbean people are more likely to suffer positional asphyxia than whites' (*The Guardian*, 1998), further suggesting that the link might be related to the presence of sickle cell in black people. Commentators noted that since the state had made no attempts to prevent deaths by issuing guidelines, then the state appeared to be using racialising biology as and when it suited its particular purpose (Ashcroft, 2006:138).

This is not an isolated occurrence within criminal justice. Dyson and Boswell (2009) trace the manner in which sickle cell trait is (mis)used in a number of cases of sudden death in custody as a sign of the alleged vulnerability of the black body: this reduces the possible culpability of guards. Conversely, they also outline how the symptoms of prisoners living with sickle cell anaemia are disregarded, leading to avoidable deaths associated with sickle cell taking place in the UK criminal justice system. These criminal justice contexts within which sickle cell is involved further deepen the association of crime with the terms race and black.

The implicit belief in skin colour as indicating a deep qualitative difference informs welfare as well as criminal justice services. Dyson *et al* (2007) found that both mothers and midwives implicitly use notions of distinct biological race at the point of the ante-natal screening when an ethnicity screening question is asked to establish whether the mother is at risk of sickle cell and the risk level. However, the scientifically accurate understanding of the relationship between social ethnicity and the risk of carrying genes associated with sickle cell, a message midwives are supposed to convey as part of providing informed choice in reproductive decision-making, disturbs this commonsense race thinking. Some midwives were prepared to override formal policy in favour of their own perceptions of who was at risk, based on notions of racial characteristics. At the heart of this challenge for health screening in a multi-ethnic society is not only an implied belief in distinct biological 'races' but an enduring belief that these races can be readily characterised by the casual observer by reference to skin colour and facial characteristics.

Similar misplaced beliefs can have deadly effects in terms of security and terrorism. In a high profile case soon after the bombings on London tubes and buses on 7 July 2005, causing the deaths of 54 people, and the day after the thwarted bombings of 21 July, Jean Charles de Menezes was killed by police as he boarded an underground train in South London. On the day of the shooting, de Menezes, of Brazilian descent, was described by an eye witness as Asian. Moreover, detectives visually confused him with Hussein Osman, an Ethiopian who was eventually found guilty of murder for the bombings. Officers referred to a similarity between Osman and de Menezes, saying both had 'Mongolian eyes' (Gillborn, 2008). The member of the public must have assumed that he could read off lineage from facial characteristics and skin colour. The police officers failed technically to distinguish between people who looked quite different, but whose similarity consisted of looking *Other*. Race thus remains a key organising feature within popular discourse both in relation to health screening and to security policing.

Community cohesion

The implementation of a national screening programme for sickle cell in England has revealed some genetic carriers who self-identify as white English. The health professionals at the forefront of counselling such carriers are women of African or African-Caribbean descent (Dyson, 2005). They re-count the challenge to white English people of carrying genes popularly associated with the other.

The reaction of some white clients is clearly racist. It falls to the sickle cell counsellors to respond to these white clients who say they feel 'polluted' because they have a so-called black gene in them (Dyson, 2005). To distance the genetic information from the negative signifiers of black African and slavery, the counsellors emphasise other plausible possibilities. They might suggest that the gene came through the Roman occupation of Britain, via the dispersal of Mediterranean sailors around the British coast following the destruction of the Spanish Armada. Or it may have come through the British Raj in India, where the haemoglobin variant D-Punjab in people of white British descent was possibly a product of the stationing of British Army personnel in that region for 200 years (Lehmann and Huntsman, 1974). The black counsellors report wistfully that they have to teach white British people their own history (Dyson, 2005).

This reaction of self-defined white English carriers of genes associated with sickle cell who describe themselves as 'tainted' by genes they associate with 'being black', suggests a persistence of scientific racism in popular discourse. This enduring race-thinking suggests fragility in contemporary community cohesion: the false belief in distinct biological race also informs the work of some health professionals, who think they can visually identify those at risk of carrying genes associated with sickle cell and police officers who think they can identify suspects based on racialised characteristics.

Conclusion

This chapter has proposed that sickle cell provides a model through which we may better understand the complexities of 21st century Europe. Historically, sickle cell and other inherited haemoglobin disorders such as thalassaemia were more associated with states in Southern Europe such as Italy, Greece, and Turkey. Current epidemiological estimates suggest that migration, differential birth rates, and inter-ethnic unions have meant that there are more affected sickle cell conceptions in Northern and Western Europe than in Southern Europe (Modell *et al*, 2007). When properly understood, therefore, sickle cell disrupts commonsense understandings of race and difference, of culture and bodies, and of peoples and place. To adequately respond to a population with higher numbers of people living with sickle cell than before requires us to search for more complex understandings, at once more individual and more group-orientated. Crucially these groups, or communities of interest, do not map neatly onto existing race groups of the popular imagination.

As we have seen, the issue of sickle cell has been mobilised as a black issue by racist commentators, especially in anti-immigration and health risks rhetoric, but also by community activists wishing to advance the case for equitable treatment for those living with sickle cell. The question is how to keep the solidarity and advocacy associated with political blackness but to lose the ideological anchoring of signifiers such as sickle cell and black by challenging the assumption of distinct biological race.

Stuart Hall (1997) once famously described race as a 'floating signifier'. Perhaps sickle cell is a floating signifier of a second order. For some it signifies black and race and in the system of meaning seems to co-notate biologically-grounded difference and inferiority by virtue of a body allegedly flawed. Thus sickle cell can be mobilised as negative signifier across all the domains of social policy discussed in this chapter. Since it is an inherited, genetic health issue, its usual role in a system of meaning is to affirm conceptions of race that are both biologically determinist and hierarchical. However, properly understood, sickle cell disrupts prevailing notions of race, signifies both diversity and connectedness, and could be a key cultural resource in framing a New Europe.

References

Adesina, AA (2007) My ordeal in unlawful immigration detention. Medical Justice Network, 30, Portland Rise, London N4 2PP http://www.medicaljustice.org.uk/library/MJinquiryJCHRSubmission. doc (accessed September 2007)

Ahmad, WIU and Atkin, K (1996) Ethnicity and caring for a disabled child: the case of sickle cell or thalassaemia, *British Journal of Social Work* 26, pp755-775

American Anthropological Association (1998) Statement on 'Race' http://www.aaanet.org/stmts/racepp.htm (accessed September 2007)

American Sociological Association (2003) *Statement of the American Sociological Association on the Importance of Collecting Data and Doing Social Scientific Research on Race* http://www2. asanet.org/media/asa_race_statement.pdf (accessed September 2007)

Anionwu, EN (1993) Sickle cell and thalassaemia: community experience and official response. In Ahmad, WIU (ed) *'Race' and Health in Contemporary Britain.* Buckingham: Open University Press

Anionwu, EN and Atkin K (2001) *The Politics of Sickle Cell and Thalassaemia.* Buckingham: Open University Press

Ashcroft, R (2006) Race in medicine: from probability to categorical practice. In Ellison, GTH and Goodman, AH (eds) *The Nature of Difference: science, society and human biology*, London: Routledge

BBC News (2000) Asylum seeker sent home in jet Monday 31st July 2000 http://news.bbc. co.uk/1/hi/uk/859416.stm (accessed September 2007)

Beckett, C (1999) Deaths in custody and the inquest system. *Critical Social Policy* 19(2) p271-280

Bhopal, R and Donaldson, L (1988) Health education for ethnic minorities: current provision and future directions. *Health Education Journal* 47(4) p 137-140

Buckner, M (2004) Sickle-cell disease: from Sierra Leone to southeast London, *The Lancet* 364 (9442) p1361

Carter, R (2007) Genes, genomes and genealogies: the return of scientific racism? *Ethnic and Racial Studies* 30(4) pp546-556

Chambers, E (2003) The art of Donald Rodney In Hylton, R (ed) *Donald Rodney: doublethink.* London: Autograph

Dennis-Antwi, J (2006) Sickle Cell in Ghana: father's reactions and perspectives, Unpublished PhD thesis, De Montfort University

Department of Health (1993) *The Report of the Working Party of the Standing Medical Advisory Committee on Sickle Cell, Thalassaemia and Other Haemoglobinopathie.* London: HMSO

Department of Health (2000) *The NHS Plan: a plan for investment, a plan for reform.* London: HMSO

Dyson, SM (2005) *Ethnicity and Screening for Sickle Cell/Thalassaemia.* Oxford: Elsevier

Dyson, SM and Boswell, GR (2009) *Sickle Cell and Deaths in Custody.* London: Whiting and Birch

Dyson, SM, Cochran, F, Culley, LA, Dyson, SE, Kennefick, A, Kirkham, M, Morris, P, Sutton, F, and Squire, P (2007) Observation and interview findings from the ethnicity questions and antenatal screening for sickle cell/thalassaemia [EQUANS] study. *Critical Public Health* 17 (1) pp31-43

Dyson, SM, Abuateya, H, Atkin, K, Culley, LA, Dyson, SE, Rowley, DT and members of the Sickle Cell and Education Group (2009) Reported school experiences of young people living with sickle cell disorder in England. *British Educational Research Journal* iFirst Article 10 July 2009, pp1-18

Franklin, I (1988) Services for sickle cell disease: unified approach needed. *British Medical Journal* 296: p592

Gillborn, D (2008) *Racism and Education: coincidence or conspiracy?* Abingdon, Oxon: Routledge

Giordano, PC, Bouva, M, and Hartefeld, CL (2005) A confidential inquiry estimating the number of patients affected with sickle cell disease and thalassemia major confirms the need for a prevention strategy in the Netherlands, *Hemoglobin* 28 (4) pp287-296

Graesdal, JS, Gundersen, K , Holm, B and Waage, A (2001) Thalassemia and sickle-cell disease in Norway. *Tidsskrt Nor Laegeforen* 121(6) p678-80

Guardian (1998) Prison boss says sorry for suffocation remark. 28 March

Gulbis, B, Ferster, A, Cotton, F, Lebouchard, MP, Cochaux, P and Fanchon, V (2006) Neonatal haemoglobinopathy screening: review of a 10-year programme in Brussels. *Journal of Medical Screening* 13(2) pp76-8

Gunaratnam, Y (2001) Ethnicity and palliative care In Culley, L. and Dyson, SM, (eds) *Ethnicity and Nursing Practice*. Basingstoke: Palgrave

Hall, S (1997) *Race: the floating signifier*. Northampton, MA: Media Education Foundation

Hall, S (2003) Preface, Hylton, R (2003) (Ed) *Donald Rodney: doublethink*. London: Autograph

Housing and Immigration Group (2006) *Written Evidence to the Joint Committee on Human Rights*. Memorandum 49, September 2006 http://www.publications.parliament.uk/pa/jt200607/jtselect/jtrights/81/81we52.htm (accessed September 2007)

Independent Media Centre UK (2008) Forced removal of suicidal sickle cell sufferer. https://www.indymedia.org.uk/media/2008/04//396057.doc (accessed April 2008)

Jones, S, Duncan, ER, Thomas, N, Walters, J, Dick, MC, Height, S, Stephens, A, Thein, Swee Lay, and Rees, D (2005) Windy weather and low humidity are associated with an increased number of hospital admissions for acute pain and sickle cell disease in an urban environment with a maritime temperate climate, *British Journal of Haematology* 131 pp530-533

Lavinha, J, Gonçalves, J, Faustino, P, Romão, L, Osório-Almeida, L, Peres, MJ, Picanço, I, Martins, MC, Ducrocq, R and Labie, D (1992) Importation route of the sickle cell trait into Portugal: contribution of molecular biology, *Human Biology* 64 pp891-901

Lawal, Omoniyi (2007) *Personal e-communication*, 27 March 2007

Lehmann, H (1963) Some medical problems of immigration into Britain: haemoglobinopathies, *Proceedings of the Royal Society of Medicine* 56(7) pp569-572

Lehmann, H and Huntsman, RG (1974) *Man's Haemoglobins*. Philadelphia: JP Lippincott, Second Edition

Modell, B, Darlison, M, Birgens, H, Cario, H, Faustino, P, Giordano, PC, Gulbis, B, Hopmeier, P, Lena-Russo, D, Romao, L, and Theodorsson, E (2007) Epidemiology of haemoglobin disorders in Europe: an overview. *Scandinavian Journal of Clinical and Laboratory Investigations* 67 pp39-70

National Coalition of Deportation Campaigns NCADC (2002) Kem and Abdul must stay http://www.ncadc.org.uk/archives/filed%20newszines/oldnewszines/newszine78/kem.html (accessed April 2008)

National Coalition of Deportation Campaigns NCADC (2005) Frank Kiore must stay http://www.ncadc.org.uk/archives/filed%20newszines/oldnewszines/newszine58/frank.htm (accessed July 2007)

National Coalition of Deportation Campaigns NCADC (2008) Helen Laolu-Balogun and children http://www.ncadc.org.uk/archives/filed%20newszines/newszine91/HelenLaolu-Balogun.html (accessed April 2008)

Nazroo, JY (1999) The racialisation of inequalities in health In Dorling, D. and Simpson, S. (eds) *Statistics in Society: the arithmetic of politics.* London: Arnold

Ohene-Frempong, K and Nkrumah, FK (1994) Sickle cell disease in Africa. In Emburey, SH, Hebbel, RP, Mohandas, N and Steinberg, MH (eds) *Sickle Cell Disease: basic principles and clinical practice.* New York: Raven Press.

Organisation for Sickle Cell Anaemia Research Netherlands (2007) Personal e-communication 21st March 2007

Prashar U, Anionwu EN and Brozovic M (1985) *Sickle Cell Anaemia: who cares?* London: Runnymede Trust

Plugge, E, Douglas, N and Fitzpatrick, R (2006) *The Health of Women in Prison*, Oxford: Department of Public Health, University of Oxford

Residents Against Racism, Ireland (2005) Grace Efe Afekhai: sick mother and child face deportation http://www.residentsagainstracism.org/?p=17 (accessed July 2007)

Roberts, I and de Montalembert, M (2007) Sickle cell disease as a paradigm of immigration haematology: new challenges for haematologists in Europe, *Haematologica* 92 (7) pp865-871

Russo-Mancuso, G, La Spina, M, and Schiliro, G (2003) The changing profile of sickle cell disease in Italy, *European Journal of Epidemiology* 8(9) pp923-924

Serjeant, GR and Sergeant, BE (2001) *Sickle Cell Disease* Third Edition, Oxford: Oxford University Press.

Sprotson, K and Nazroo, JY (eds) (2002) *Ethnic Minority Psychiatric Illness Rates in the Community (EMPIRIC) – Quantitative Report.* London: The Stationery Office

Thomas-Hope, EM (1992) International migration and health: sickle cell and thalassaemia care in the United Kingdom. *GeoJournal* 26(1) pp75-79

UNESCO (1950) *The Race Question: text of the statement issued 18th July 1950.* Paris: UNESCO

World Health Organisation (1988) The Haemoglobinopathies in Europe: combined report of two WHO meetings (Document EUR/ICP/MCH 110) Copenhagen: WHO Regional Office for Europe

Yallop, D, Duncan, ER, Norris, E, Fuller, GW, Thomas, N, Walters, J, Dick, MC, Height, S, Stephens, A, Thein, SL and Rees, D (2007) The associations between air quality and the number of hospital admissions for acute pain and sickle-cell disease in an urban environment. *British Journal of Haematology* 136(6) p844-848

Yates, SJ, Dyson, SM and Payne, M (2009) Children and young people in hospitals: doing youth work in medical settings. *Journal of Youth Studies* 12(1) pp1-16

5

Restrictionalism versus Liberalism? The rupture between asylum and integration in the EU

Jenny Phillimore

Introduction

Until comparatively recently most refugees arrived in the EU under the auspices of refugee programmes set up in response to international action pertaining to particular global political issues, for example the so-called Bosnian crisis, Vietnamese boat-people or the expulsion of Asians from Uganda (Sales, 2002; Kuepper *et al*, 1975:9). It was not until the 1990s that the numbers of asylum applicants arriving spontaneously as individuals began to increase to the extent that successive governments felt the need to create policy initiatives to address the influx.

The past ten years have seen the arrival of large numbers of people seeking asylum in the EU and the UK in particular, with figures reaching an all time high in 2002. In response to the pressure that supporting these asylum seekers was placing on services in Southern England, the National Asylum Support Service (NASS), now the UK Border Agency, was set up in 1999 to co-ordinate and fund dispersal of asylum seekers around the UK. A raft of policies designed to ensure that asylum seekers could not 'take advantage of the system' and were no longer attracted to the UK, accompanied the establishment of dispersal. Over time, government policy increasingly focused upon excluding asylum seekers from UK society and marking them as 'undeserving' while giving little support for the integration of asylum seekers who passed through the system and gained the right to remain in the UK (Sales, 2002).

This chapter considers the impact of restrictionalist asylum policy, which explicitly excludes asylum seekers from society, and liberal integration policy, which takes a *laissez faire* approach to refugees' ability to integrate into life in the EU. It explores academic and policy understandings of integration and the notion that integration begins at arrival. Using data collected from a range of studies across the West Midlands region of the UK, the chapter examines the impacts of current asylum policy upon refugees' integration. It concludes by suggesting that there is a rupture between asylum and integration policy and that there are clear indications that the exclusion sanctioned during the asylum period undermines the ability of refugees to integrate. A number of measures are suggested to help mitigate the effects the asylum seeking experience.

Restrictionalism and asylum

Applications for asylum in the EU began to rise at the end of the 1980s peaking at over 800,000 per annum in 1992 (UNHCR, 2009) and continuing to rise in the UK from 37,000 in 1996 to a peak of 103,080 per annum in 2002 (Home Office, 2003). In 2001/02 the UK spent £1015 million on asylum support and more people applied for asylum in the UK than any other EU country (*Guardian*, 2.5.2003). Controls on the legal entry of immigrants, such as the issuing of national visas and introduction of carriers' liability, to Europe, through the EU and other intergovernmental arrangements, the so-called fortress Europe, have meant that asylum is often the only means of gaining access to Europe (Sales, 2002; Bloch and Schuster, 2002). Britain has become one of the major proponents of the EU's growing restrictionism towards asylum seekers erecting barriers to entry and introducing changes to the social support system for asylum seekers, which make them more visible as a group and re-enforce public perceptions of them being a burden, reliant on 'state handouts' (Zetter and Pearl, 2000; Sales, 2002).

Politics and asylum are inextricably linked in the EU. The UK's 2005 General Election campaign provided an excellent example of how migrants are used as ammunition in an attempt by both main political parties to score points for being the toughest against illegal immigration and bogus asylum seekers. Labour kicked off its campaign with the publication of the Government's Five Year Asylum and Immigration Strategy (February, 2005) setting out some measures described by the Refugee Council (2005) as having 'serious implications for the future of asylum in the UK'. These included suggestions, some of which have now been implemented, to review an individual's refugee status after five years, fast track removals of failed asylum seekers, and increase detention. The report of the Council of Europe's Racism Commission found that the xenophobic attitude evident in the British media, political debate and government policy exacerbated intolerance amongst the general population (ECRI, 2005). Racism directed at refugees and asylum seekers in Britain was considered to be particularly acute. A review of literature by Hubbard (2005) revealed suggestions that anxieties about the 'flood' of asylum seekers had triggered draconian measures designed to protect the boundaries of the nation. The media depiction of asylum seekers as a social, welfare and security problem, encouraged this boundary protection further (Bloch and Schuster, 2002:398).

The massive increase in arrivals and the negative media coverage were followed by several pieces of legislation aimed at 'securing our borders' (Home Office, 2002). This legislation, the first aimed specifically at asylum seekers, was followed by what is described by the Refugee Council as a 'phenomenal' pace of legal developments. The Home Office (1998) white paper *Firmer, Faster, Fairer* suggested restricting both social and financial benefits to create a deterrent. This paper, originally produced by the right-wing Conservative administration, was introduced by centre-left New Labour who took office in the same year. The 1999 Immigration and Asylum Act removed all benefit entitlement for asylum seekers and created the National Asylum Support Service (NASS), now renamed the UK Borders Agency (UKBA). This Act made entry to the UK harder by introducing fines for carriers of £2000 per illegal immigrant. NASS began operating in April 2000. It provided a basic package of support for destitute asylum seekers equivalent to 70 per cent of income support. Those without access to housing were dispersed to accommodation in the dispersal regions outside London. Areas were located on the basis of housing availability and concerns were expressed about the lack of support services to help asylum seekers deal with their immigration claims and indeed their everyday life.

The secondary aim of the 1999 Immigration and Asylum Act was to make asylum in the UK less attractive to asylum seekers, a theme which was to be developed further in the legislation that followed. The Nationality, Asylum and Immigration Act 2002 placed further emphasis on the control and removal of unsuccessful applicants. Detention centres were renamed 'removal' centres, and rights to appeal were reduced. This Act removed the right of applicants to work or undertake vocational training and widened the range of measures aimed at reducing illegal working, including allowing immigration officers to enter a place of work without a warrant and to levy fines of up to £5000.

The 2004 Asylum and Immigration Act legislated for a 'local connection' in requiring only those authorities where an individual was housed as an asylum seeker to support their claim for social housing once they received leave to remain. This made it difficult for refugees to move around the UK in search of employment or to re-unite with family settled elsewhere. The Immigration, Asylum and Nationality Bill (2005) introduced on the spot fines for those found to be employing illegal workers. In a further blow the then DFES announced that from September 2007 asylum seekers would be excluded from further education and ESOL and that fee remission would only be available for refugees in receipt of benefit. This was later revised so asylum seekers waiting more than six months for a decision on their case could access ESOL.

As we have seen over time, the UK Government's stance on asylum has hardened to the point where Zetter and Pearl (2000:680) argue that the whole asylum process is intended to disenfranchise asylum seekers from society:

> as state benefits are reduced and the asylum regime becomes more an instrument of marginalisation than reception, of community fragmentation than consolidation, of short-term dependency than long term sufficiency.

Whilst evidence mounts that it is not asylum seekers who determine their destination but the people smugglers who have become their only route away from persecution. Policies in the UK have led the trend in Europe to becoming increasingly restrictionist as measures have been introduced which reduce access to benefits, learning, employment and accommodation (Robinson and Segrott, 2002; Bloch and Schuster, 2002; Bloch, 1999; Sales, 2002). These policies present an image of the UK being an unreceptive and unattractive destination for asylum seekers.

The role of integration

Whilst the raft of legislation introduced throughout the 1990s and 2000s mainly acted to reduce the rights of asylum seekers, the EU has sought to facilitate refugee integration in member states by introducing transnational funding streams such as EQUAL and the European Refugee Fund. Before exploring these policies it is worth considering what is meant by the term integration. Integration is a much contested term and one that has been subject to a great deal of debate (Castles *et al*, 2002). Berry (1997) argues that integration is one of the four possible acculturation strategies open to newcomers. Assimilation occurs when individuals do not wish to maintain their cultural identity and seek daily interaction with other cultures. Separation takes place when individuals prioritise holding on to their original culture and avoid interaction with others. Marginalisation is likely when there is little interest in cultural maintenance or in having relationships with others, possibly because of a sense of exclusion. Finally integration occurs when there is an interest in both maintaining one's original culture while engaging in daily interactions with others. Integration is argued to be the most positive approach to adaptation in that it is likely to involve the least amount of psychological trauma to the migrant population (Berry, 1997). However integration can only be pursued when the dominant society is open and inclusive towards cultural diversity (Berry, 1991). The importance of mutual adaptation is one of the key themes that emerge from the literature.

Integration is sometimes discussed in terms of different components, dimensions or indicators in a bid to try to find some mechanisms by which to explore migrants' progress towards integration. Whilst this approach has been criticised because it makes accounting for the multi-faceted, interlinking and non-linear nature of the integration process difficult, it is useful to help us to explore the different aspects of society and how they impact on the ability to integrate (Castles *et al*, 2002; Fyvie *et al*, 2003). Zetter and Griffith *et al*'s review of integration policy in the EU (2002) found that there were four dimensions that influenced integration. These comprise actions and experiences as well as access to services. The first dimension is legal status and citizenship and recognises that both the length of time awaiting a decision and the experience of the process of asylum seeking can influence the ability to integrate once a positive decision is received. Once status is granted the nature of statutory integration support, strategies, and policy also influence the process. Clearly the support refugees are given to aid their integration will influence their ability to access the functional aspects of integration. These are often viewed by policymakers and academics as the key dimensions of the process and include access to education, employment, and housing amongst other services (Bloch, 2002). The final dimension, social integration, tends to be overlooked in state integration programmes: it comprises participation in social networks.

The UK's National Refugee Integration Forum (NRIF) was introduced following *Full and Equal Citizens* (Home Office, 2000), with the aim of exploring mechanisms to help refugee integration. The 2002 Act increased competitive funding for projects that addressed specific social needs amongst refugee communities. However funding levels remained low and the changes were criticised as being insignificant. Two integration strategies, *Integration Matters* (Home Office) and *Working to Rebuild Lives* (DWP), were released in March, 2005. Integration Matters listed the range of problems that needed to be addressed and proposed some solutions. Much emphasis is placed upon helping refugees to achieve their full potential and the need to provide opportunities for language training, early contact with Jobcentre Plus, work experience, retraining and accreditation. Importance was placed upon mobilising the voluntary sector, the Challenge Fund and the NRIF in helping refugees to achieve these goals. In addition the piloting of a Strategic Upgrade of National Refugee Integration Services known, as the SUNRISE initiative in four areas across the UK, was announced.

The initiative enabled new refugees to work with a caseworker to create a Personal Integration Plan. *Working to Rebuild Lives* (DWP, 2005) discussed the need to develop partnerships to help in the creation of services for refugees and sets out plans to encourage refugees to undertake Basic Skills and ESOL training and to enhance the support on offer in Jobcentres. Neither integration strategy had designated resources to aid their implementation.

In 2006, in what can only be viewed as a retrograde step in the development of integration policy, the NRIF, the only organisation charged with reviewing progress on refugee integration, was dissolved. At the same time it was announced that all integration funds would be channelled into a new National Refugee Integration Service now termed the Refugee Integration and Employment Service (RIES). This service would signpost new refugees, who had gained status from 2008, to existing education, learning and housing provision, rather than developing new initiatives *per se*. RCOs and NGOs expressed concern at the withdrawal of Home Office funding from their sector. In addition the logic of providing a service only for new refugees was questioned, given the evidence that refugees required support far beyond the first six months after receiving their status.

Many commentators argue that integration is a long term process which starts with arrival and ends when refugees are active members of society from a legal, social, economic and cultural perspective (Schibel *et al*, 2002; Castles *et al*, 2002; Fyvie *at al*, 2003). The Government in the UK aims to ensure that 'integration can only begin in its fullest sense when an asylum seeker becomes a refugee' (Home Office, 2005:3). The asylum process can take anywhere between one day and over a decade. In 2003 there was said to be a backlog of 60,000 claims (Bourn, 2004) and in 2007 the Home Office commenced a review of over 460,000 legacy cases, many concerning families who had been in the UK for several years. With many individuals spending years as asylum seekers, it is important to consider the impact of restrictionalist policies on those who eventually gain refugee status. Evidence presented by

Cantle (2002) on the riots which took place in Northern British towns during 2001 suggests that the experience of many first, second and even third generation immigrants in the UK is marginalisation rather than integration and that there is a need for active intervention to ensure that integration and cohesion can take place. The chapter will use qualitative data collected from 192 interviews with refugees living in the West Midlands) to explore the impact of legal and statutory dimensions of asylum and integration policy upon refugees' ability to integrate in functional and social dimensions (Phillimore and Goodson, 2005).

Functional integration: employment, Education and ESOL

The interviewees saw education as the key to integration because they recognised that they would be unable to work until they could speak some English and have their overseas skills and qualifications recognised. The majority had experienced difficulties accessing ESOL:

> When I came to this country, I didn't know anybody and had lots of problems. I went to register to a college but the college didn't accept me and they asked me to come next year. From that time I go to college. Over one year I was waiting for the course .(Afghanistan male, 17)

Respondents also expressed concern about the quality of ESOL lessons with many finding the teaching poor. Refugees were expected to learn in crowded, mixed ability classes, with the level pitched at those of lowest ability

> Every time I attend the classes, I found out that I have gone beyond that level ... sometime the teachers would just teach the same thing, it was difficult to learn anything new. So, I stopped going. (Ethiopian male, 34)

Satisfaction and achievement in ESOL were very low. Only those who were seeking basic conversational language had achieved their aims in any number. Only 22.5 per cent of those who wanted to learn English to access work or further education achieved their aims. Drop out rates were extremely high. Those who had started ESOL as asylum seekers found the stress associated with awaiting a decision, combined with lack of income and no access to Learner Support Funds, made studying difficult. Mental health problems were a significant issue for a proportion of respondents

> I can no longer sleep well, I have insomnia, I dream that I am in war, I see what was happening and I have headaches. I am no longer able to concentrate on things as I used to be. (Congolese male)

No courses were available to help students get their qualifications recognised. Skilled and professional refugees were told by colleges and by Jobcentre Plus that they would have to begin their studies again. However the majority of refugees were excluded from full-time education either by their language ability or by the need to comply with a ruling from Jobcentre Plus, the UK labour office, which meant they would be ineligible for benefits if they studied in excess of 16 hours per week. In reality most respondents were unlikely to gain work commensurate with their skills or ability. Studies looking at refugee employment levels in the West Midlands have found that unemployment rates exceeded 60 per cent (Phillimore *et al*, 2003). Certainly our interviewees struggled to access employment with only 20.5 per cent of respondents employed since their arrival in the UK and all, regardless of their employment history, being employed in low skilled, temporary work. Research undertaken with employers revealed that they were reluctant to engage refugees because they were concerned that they might live up to their media image of being unskilled, 'lazy' or 'criminal' (Hurstfield *et al*, 2004; Phillimore and Goodson, 2008). They were also worried about the ways in which language difficulties might impact on safety or productivity and how skills gained overseas would equate to the skills they needed. Finally they lacked knowledge about methods of determining individuals' legal right to work, were nervous about accidentally transgressing rules and fearful of being fined.

Social integration

Lack of language ability was the single biggest factor in preventing refugees from interacting with the host population. One woman would not venture out without an escort: 'if I get lost I cannot find my way' (Somali, 70) whilst another was dependent on people whenever she needed to access services: 'I rely on interpreter and friends wherever I go' (Somali, 26). Individuals restricted to informal networks comprising members from their own ethnic groups enjoyed the support and knowledge they received from their friends. Only half of respondents had any contact whatsoever with local people, largely with neighbours, parents at school, retail workers and colleagues. Just four people had what they described as social contact where they elected to spend time together. Two thirds of interviewees were unable to move beyond their communities. Over half of respondents were keen to have some form of social contact with local people from outside their ethnic community, in order to gain knowledge about how to live within wider UK society, and make new friends, but they were constrained by lack of opportunity, language and fear.

Refugees' experience of the asylum process often left them feeling unwanted and stigmatised. On seeking asylum they soon realised that they had to demonstrate that they were 'genuine' refugees. For many having to re-tell their story was extremely stressful, their distress increased when they were told that they had made their stories up:

> First of all the war I went through, the way people have been killed, the way a body is opened up from the stomach, it is not a story, I have seen it myself. From what I have seen in my country and the way we are treated in this country it is double. I had all those immigration troubles to add to my experience of war. Then I felt mentally ill (Congolese male)

Being detained on arrival had traumatised several of the respondents. Detention echoed experiences of imprisonment in their countries of origin and made them question the fairness of the system:

> For instance, where I was back home, the reason that made me run away I was in a situation where I was hiding myself. And for me to go through that and come all the way here, again you are taken into detention. (Kenyan woman, 39)

Being compelled to sign in at their local police station made asylum seekers feel like criminals. The fear they experienced entering the police station was coupled with low self-esteem and impacted on their mental health.

Respondents all struggled with the uncertainty of their situation when going through the asylum process.

> I was worried and anxious about my future in this country. I wondered if they were going to grant refugee status to me or deport me from this country. I will never forget the anxieties and the fears that I had when I was waiting for an answer and I will never forget those nights I could not sleep. All these things had negative effects on me. (Iranian male, 47)

Until they arrived, many had no idea that there was any question of not being allowed to remain. The threat of deportation meant they lived in fear of returning to possibly grave situations. Several respondents knew people who had committed suicide rather than live in uncertainty. Asylum seekers often waited years for a decision, all the time fearing they would be unsuccessful, and would lose NASS support as many had seen friends made destitute and homeless once their appeals were exhausted. Lives were put on hold; people could not make plans, and 'lost hope'. Unable to work, they spent their days with no purposeful activity and endless time to worry about the future and the well-being of their remaining family back home.

The asylum system left those gaining a positive decision feeling unwanted. One third of respondents reported experiencing harassment. Incidents varied from verbal to physical attacks. There were a number of dimensions to the discrimination experienced. The image propagated by the media of asylum seekers as criminals, terrorists and liars undermined their self-esteem:

> Refugees have been portrayed as people who come to take money. We are stressed because people don't like us. Our community stressed because of being refugee, black and African. (Congolese male, 30)

Secondly, they were not welcomed by the host population in the neighbourhoods to which they were dispersed. This made them feel isolated from society as well as disenfranchised by the state. The combination of institutional and societal discrimination excluded them from mechanisms that may have served to integrate them or at least provide support and advice:

> I was hoping to be welcomed and to be taken care of, because when you flee your country, you hope that you will get people to welcome you and understand and feel sympathy of what you went through. But I did not get that. It makes it difficult to integrate into society. (Zimbabwean woman, 40)

Refugees living in the UK found 'the rules' unclear. They felt unsure about what they are able to do because racism in the UK is hidden 'but it is still here killing people inside'. Refugees felt that they were shunned by people in their neighbourhood:

> Some people see you differently as an asylum seeker and they would keep distance from us or being not friendly. (Albanian woman, 32)

> There are some fears. Some are being bullied. When the people are bullied, they think that they are not wanted in the community ... When people are looking at you, you are thinking that you are not welcomed. (Afghani woman, 25)

Some of the respondents stated that their children suffered from mistreatment and discrimination which led to them restricting the freedom of their children:

> My children are prisoners in their bedroom, because, I am afraid of the fact that they are racially abused by other children. (Sudanese woman, 36)

Some refugee children were truanting from school to avoid harassment. One respondent described how her child was excluded from school for hitting another pupil. On examination she discovered the 'victim' had, in the full knowledge of a teacher, been racially abusing her son; only after concerted action was she able to have the racism acknowledged as a problem. The negative image of refugees in the media exacerbated feelings of inferiority and rejection. Some were ashamed of their identity, being a refugee, and the stigma attached to it.

> People don't take refugees as human being. I am ashamed to say that I am a refugee. (Rwandan male, 22)

Inability to speak English, or the fact that they spoke English with an accent was a further factor that marked refugees as different and prevented communication with local people:

> How other people treat you especially when you do not speak English is not good. (Chad woman, 18)

> First of all when you come to a different country, you don't speak English. When you cannot express yourself, the door is closed, the window is closed. So, there is a huge barrier between you and the community. (Afghani male, 31)

Over time these experiences and the lack of positive opportunities to communicate with local people led to a situation where it could be argued some refugees became separate from local communities, rather than integrated into them and withdrew from the very activities that might offer opportunities to integrate:

> The house is very old, it's really horrible and the neighbours unfriendly ... we keep ourselves to ourselves, there is fighting in the neighbourhood, a lot of trouble and sometimes racism on the estates so we stay in ... I have even stopped going to college now. (Rwandan female, 34)

Discussion and conclusions

Evidence presented in this chapter indicates that restrictionalist asylum policy had a negative impact on individuals' ability to integrate in the UK. Further research is needed to explore the extent to which the exclusionary effect of asylum policy differs between ethnic groups or individuals awaiting a decision for different periods of time. It is clear that asylum seekers are aware that they are 'unwanted'. The questioning of their stories, the fight to gain status and treatment as criminals rather than persons in need of humanitarian assistance, combined with clear messages from the media that asylum seekers are not only unwanted but criminal or, post 9/11, even terrorist, all re-enforced this view. There was also evidence that local communities and employers in dispersal areas had reacted to negative representations of asylum seekers to make them targets of harassment or discrimination. As a result asylum seekers and refugees sought to avoid interaction and withdrew into their own ethnic groups or into isolation becoming marginalised, or separated, from the mainstream. In this way asylum policy mitigated against the development of social capital that is so important for integration and cohesion. At the present time there is no mechanism in place to encourage or facilitate interaction.

There is plenty of evidence that ESOL is not fit for purpose and that under the current system newcomers are not able to learn the language they need to communicate, or to gain citizenship (Grover, 2006). The withdrawal of free ESOL for many asylum seekers can only exacerbate these problems. Individuals will have less time to learn English before gaining refugee status and those asylum seekers who continue to remain, often indefinitely, will be totally reliant on interpreters. Without the ability to speak English refugees will not be able to access the learning they need to progress and will find gaining work difficult. The longer they remain unemployed, the less desirable they are as employees. Exclusion from learning as asylum seekers and the absence of initiatives to recognise refugees' skills or qualifications, to offer opportunities for work experience or vocational training, is a problem for refugees wanting to gain access to work. This *laissez faire* approach to developing refugee employability stands in stark contrast to the approaches taken in Scandinavia and Northern Europe, where skills recognition systems and work experience programmes have been developed and resourced centrally (Phillimore *et al*, 2005). The Dutch experience has demonstrated that work experience and apprenticeship programmes can help to ensure that refugees gain access to the labour market (Scheldler and Glastra, 2000).

The discussion of asylum and integration policy has demonstrated a rupture between restrictionist asylum policy and liberal integration policy. Immigration policy marks asylum seekers as undeserving and fundamentally not part of UK society. Having made concerted effort to marginalise asylum seekers through ensuring that they do not develop relationships with employers, trainers and to some extent the local population. The expectation that as refugees they should, with limited support and no adaptation in institutional structures, suddenly be able to develop relationships with the dominant population is unrealistic. On the one hand Government expresses concern about the lack of social cohesion in some deprived areas and the ghettoisation and ethnic divisions highlighted in the Cantle report, while on the other no action is taken about the growing numbers of unemployed, disenfranchised, refugees in those same areas. Whilst a House of Commons committee (2003) warned of the likelihood of a breakdown in social cohesion in dispersal areas, the main concern was about the reaction of the indigenous population to large influxes of immigrants, rather than the likely exclusion and disaffection of thousands of educated – but unemployed – refugees.

Official emphasis has been placed on reducing asylum applications and reforming the dispersal system and not on developing policy or initiatives to engage the refugees who are set to become permanent UK residents. Whilst refugees are encouraged to take citizenship training to learn about British values and culture, there is no consideration about how institutional structures might need to change in order to take into account the needs of migrants. Yet commentators are clear: integration is a two-way process involving mutual accommodation and the development of mechanisms to ensure that newcomers have equal access to all of society's resources (Berry, 1991; 1997). Until orientation is bi-directional the likelihood of integration is low and the probability that refugees will join the marginalised communities identified by Cantle is high.

Perhaps most worrying in both social exclusion and integration terms is the impact that an influx of unemployed minorities on the attitudes of the indigenous population. Wilson (1998) argues that at times of economic uncertainty people turn to what they can rationalise and that is often the voice of conservative spokespersons who speak in sound bites. Certainly in the UK there is evidence that deprived dispersal areas have succumbed to this divisiveness. A report to the UN Human Rights Committee 'blamed politicians for encouraging racist hostility in their public attitudes towards asylum seekers' (Bloch and Schuster, 2002:458). In local government elections the British National Party won a record number of seats, some in key dispersal cities. The Commission on Integration and Cohesion concluded that integration is integral to social cohesion in deprived areas (2007). They argue that it can be achieved by finding ways of facilitating meaningful interaction and dialogue and improving conditions for all.

The legal and statutory dimensions of integration identified by Zetter and Griffith *et al* (2000) underpin refugees' ability to integrate in the functional and social dimensions. It is important to ensure that the costs of integration are covered centrally before the social and economic costs of marginalisation or separation are felt locally, regionally and nationally. Creating initiatives across the EU to improve the employability of asylum seekers and refugees would represent a major advance. A starting point would be revoking bans on asylum seekers working, so as to ensure that those who gain refugee status do not become long-term unemployed as soon as they are eligible to work. A further measure would involve allowing asylum seekers to access the full range of language learning and further education opportunities from arrival, and improving the quality of language provision and the development of learning and skills recognition opportunities for new arrivals. Some EU states already invest heavily in language and employability training and find that this approach speeds integration (Phillimore, 2008).

Evidence suggests that the active and explicit exclusion of asylum seekers impacts upon their ability to integrate when they become refugees. It is difficult to argue for the abolition of immigration controls, although this case has been made by organisations such as JCWI and PICUM, but there is certainly a need for a more humanitarian approach to asylum across the EU. Decision making needs to be fast, clear and transparent and to avoid the criminalisation of asylum seekers through detention or the use of regular reporting. Asylum in particular, and immigration more generally, needs to be depoliticised and policy developed in a rational manner separate from electioneering. Responsible media coverage and the reporting of positive news stories about asylum seekers and refugees need to be encouraged to highlight the reality of the experience of asylum seeking and the struggles refugees face when trying to integrate. Finally, having successfully excluded asylum seekers from society, it is unrealistic to expect integration to happen without the development of proactive policy. Proactive integration policy, might be based upon Scandinavian models, and would entail the provision of well-resourced, specialist services available to all refugees and the development of opportunities to facilitate social interaction from the workplace to the community.

References

Aldridge, F and Waddington, S (2001) *Asylum seekers' skills and qualifications audit pilot project*, Leicester: National Organisation for Adult Learning

Anon (2003) 5 tough questions about asylum: Britain is a soft touch for asylum seekers. *Guardian* May 1 2003

Arulampalam, W and Booth, A (1998) labour market flexibility and skills acquistition: is their a trade off? (In Atkinson, A and Hills, J ed.s) *Exclusion, Employment and Opportunity* CASE paper 4. London: LSE pp65-85

Atkinson, A (1998) Social exclusion, poverty and unemployment (In Atkinson, A. and Hills, J. eds) *Exclusion, Employment and Opportunity*, CASE paper 4 London: LSE pp1-24

Berry, JW (1991) Psychology of acculturation: Understanding individuals moving between cultures (In Brislin, R ed. *Applied cross-cultural psychology, Cross-cultural research and Methodology Series* 14, pp232-253, USA: Sage

Berry, JW (1997) Immigration, Acculturation and Adaptation, in *Applied Psychology: An International Review*, Vol 46, No. 1, pp5-68

Berthoud, R (2000) Ethnic employment penalties in Britain, *Journal of Ethnic and Migration Studies*, Vol. 26, No. 3, pp389-416

Bloch, A (1999) Refugees in the job market: a case of unused skills in the British Economy, in Bloch, A and Levy, C, *Refugees, citizenship and policy in Europe,* Basingstoke: Palgrave, pp187-210

Bloch, A (2000) Refugee settlement in Britain: the impact of policy on participation. *Journal of Ethnic and Migration Studies* 26 no 1:75-88

Bloch, A (2002) *Refugees' opportunities and barriers in employment and training*, DWP Research Report series 179

Bloch, A and L Schuster (2002) Asylum and welfare: contemporary debates, in *Critical Social Policy,* Vol. 22, No. 3, pp393-414

Bourn, J (2004) *Improving the Speed and Quality of Asylum Decisions*, London, ICAR

Brochmann, G (1999) Controlling immigration in Europe in Brochmann, G and Hammar, T (eds) *Mechanisms of immigration control: a comparative analysis of European Regulation Policies.* Oxford: Berg

Burgess, S and Propper, C (2002) The dynamics of poverty. In Hills, Le Grand and and Piachaud eds (2002) *Understanding social exclusion*, Oxford OUP

Cantle, T (2002) *Community cohesion: a report of the independent review team*, London: Home Office

Carey-Wood, J (1997) *Meeting Refugees' Needs in Britain: the role of refugee-specific initiatives*, London: Home Office

Castles, S, Korac, M, Vasta, M and Vertovec, S (2002) *Integration Mapping the Field*, Oxford: Oxford University

Crick, B (2003) *The New and the Old: interim report for consultation of the 'life in the United Kingdom' Advisory Group*, London: Home Office

Commission on Integration and Cohesion (2007) *Our Shared Future*, Commission on Integration and Cohesion

Coussey, M (2000) *Framework of integration policies*, Director general III-Social Cohesion, Strasbourg: Council of Europe Publishing

ECRI (2005) *Third report on the United Kingdom.* Strasborg: European Commission Against Racism and Intolerance

European Commission (2001) *Report of the third European Conference on the integration of refugees,* Brussels: European Commission

Evans, M (2001) *Welfare to work and the organisation of opportunity: Lessons from abroad.* Case paper 15. London: LSE

Feeney, A (2000) Refugee Employment, in *Local Economy*, Vol. 15, No. 4, pp343-349

Franz, B (2003) Bosnian refugee and socio-economic realities: changes in refugee and settlement policies in Austria and the United States, *Journal of Ethnic and Migration Studies* 29 no 1: 5-25

Fyvie, A, Ager, A, Curley, G and Korac, M (2003) *Integration Mapping the Field Volume II: distilling policy lessons from the 'mapping the field' exercise,* Home Office Online Report 29/03

Gowricharn, R (2002) Integration and social cohesion: the case of the Netherlands in *Journal of Ethnic and Migration Studies* Vol. 28, 2, pp259-273

Haque, R (2003) *Migrants in the UK: a descriptive analysis of their characteristics and labour market performance, based upon the Labour Force Survey*, London: DWP

Home Office (1998) *Firmer, faster, fairer: a modern approach to immigration and asylum*, London: HMSO

Home Office (2000) *Full and Equal Citizens: a strategy for the integration of refugees into the United Kingdom*, London: HMSO

Home Office (2002) *Secure Borders Safe Haven: Integration with diversity in modern Britain,* London: HMSOHome Office (2003) Asylum Statistics, United Kingdom: HMSO

Home Office (2005) *Integration matters: national strategy for refugee integration,* London: HMSO

House of Commons Home Affairs Committee (2003) *Asylum removals,* Fourth Report of Session 2002-2003

Hubbard, P (2005) Acommodating otherness: anti-asylum centre protest and the mainenance of white privilege. *Transactions of the Institute of British Geographers.* 30 (1) pp52-65

Hurstfield, J Pearson, R, Hooker, H, Ritchie, H and Sinclair, A (2004) *Employing Refugees, Some Organisations' Experiences.* Institute for Employment Studies Paper for the Employability Forum

Immigration and Nationality Directorate (2003) *Asylum statistics: United Kingdom,* London: HMSO

INTEGRA (undated) *Combating Social Exclusion: A comparative study of Bosnian, Kurdish, Somali and Senegalese Communities in the UK, Germany, Denmark and Italy*

IPPR (2003) *States of conflict: causes and patterns of forced migration to the EU and policy responses,* London: IPPR

Joly, D (1996) *Haven or hell: asylum policy in Europe.* London: Macmillan

Knox, K (1997) *A credit to the nation: a study of refugees in the United Kingdom,* London: refugee Council

Kuepper, WG, Lackey, G L and Swinterton, E N (1975) *Ugandan Asians in Great Britain. Forced Migration and Social Absorbtion,* London: Croom Helm

mbA (1999) *Creating the conditions for refugees to find work,* Report for the Refugee Council, London

Menz, G (2002) Patterns in EU labour immigration policy: national initiatives and European responses, *Journal of Ethnic and Migration Studies* 28 no 4 pp723-742

Mestheneos, E and Ioannidi, E (2002) Obstacles to Refugee Integration in the European Union Member States, in *Journal of Refugee Studies,* Vol.15, No. 3, pp304-320.

Midlands Refugee Council (2001) *Asylum Seekers: Developing Information, Advice and Guidance on Employment, Training and Education in the West Midlands,* EQUAL bid July 2001

Morris, L (2002) Britain's asylum and immigration regime: the shifting contours of rights, *Journal of Ethnic and Migration Studies* 28 no 3: pp409-425

Nevin, B, Lee, P, Goodson, L, Murie, A and Phillimore, J (2000) *Changing housing markets and urban regeneration in the M62 Corridor,* Centre for Urban and Regional Studies: Birmingham

Nevin, B, Lee, P, Murie, A, Goodson, L and Phillimore, J (2001) *Changing housing markets and urban regeneration in the West Midlands,* Centre for Urban and Regional Studies: Birmingham

Ogbonna, E (1998) British ethnic minorities and employment training: redressing or extending disadvantage? *International Journal of Training and Development,* Vol.2, No.1, pp28-41

Phillimore, J and Goodson, L (2001) *Exploring the integration of asylum seekers and refugees in Wolverhampton into UK labour market,* Centre for Urban and Regional Studies. University of Birmingham

Phillimore, J and Goodson, L (2002) *Asylum seeker and refugee employability initiatives: models for implementing a super pathway in the West Midlands,* Discussion paper prepared for West Midlands Executive Consortia

Phillimore, J and Goodson, L (2005) *West Midlands Regional Housing Strategy West Midlands Regional Spatial Strategy Shared Evidence Base Asylum seekers and refugees,* Report for the Regional Housing Board

Phillimore, J (2008) Employability initiatives for refugees in the EU: building on good practice in McKay, S ed. *Refugees, Recent migrants and Employment,* London: Routledge

Phillimore, J and Goodson, L (2008) *New migrants in the UK: education, employment and training*, London: Trentham

Phillimore, J, Goodson, L and Oosthuizen, R (2003) *Asylum seekers and refugees: education, training, employment, skills and services in Coventry and Warwickshire*, Learning and Skills Council Coventry and Warwickshire: Coventry

Preece, J and Walters, N (1999) Accommodating refugee identity transitions: how adult education hinders or helps refugee lifelong learning needs, in '*The Final Frontier – Exploring Spaces in the Education of Adults*', University of Warwick: SCUTREA

Refugee Council (1997) *Just existence: The lives of asylum seekers who have lost entitlement to benefits in the UK*. Refugee Council: London

Refugee Council (2002) *Refugees in today's world*. Refugee Council Briefing: London

Refugee Council (2003) *Response to Home Office Consultation on Juxtaposed Controls Implementation*, Dover-Calais November 2002, Refugee Council Policy paper: London

Refugee Council (2005) *The Government's five year asylum and immigration strategy*. Refugee Council Briefing February 2005

Robinson, V. (1998) The Importance of Information in the Resettlement of Refugees in the UK in *Journal of Refugee Studies*, Vol. 11, No. 2, pp146-160

Robinson, V and Segrott, J (2002) *Understanding the decision making of asylum seekers*. Home Office Research Study 243, Home Office: London

Sales, R and Gregory, J (1996) Employment, Citizenship and European Integration: The implications for Migrant and Refugee Women in *Social Politics*, Vol. 3, pp331-351

Sales, R. (2002) The deserving and the undeserving? Refugees, asylum seekers and welfare in Britain, in *Critical Social Policy*, Vol. 22, No. 3, pp456-478

Sargeant, G and Forna, A (2001) *A Poor Reception: Refugees and Asylum Seekers: Welfare or Work?* Policy Paper, London: The Industrial Society

Schedler, P and Glastra, F (2000) Adult Education between Cultural Assimilation and Structural Integration. Settlement programmes for 'newcomers' in The Netherlands, in *Compare*, Vol. 30, No. 1, pp53-66

Schibel, Y (2002) Refugee Integration: Can research synthesis inform policy? Feasibility study report, RDS ON-line Report 13/02

Scottish Refugee Council (2001) *Responding to the needs of asylum seekers*, Glasgow: Scottish Refugee Council

Shields, MA and Wheatley Price, S (2003) *The labour market outcomes and psychological well-being of ethnic minority migrants in Britain*, Home Office Online Report 07/03

Social Trends (2002) Unemployment rates: by region, 2002: *Social Trends* 33

Srinivasan, S (1994) *An overview of research into refugee groups in Britain during the 1990s*. Paper presented at 4th International Research and Advisory Panel Conference, Oxford cited in Bloch, A (1999) Refugees in the job market: a case of unused skills in the British Economy, in Bloch, A and Levy, C *Refugees, citizenship and policy in Europe*, Basingstoke: Palgrave, pp187-210

Thomas, F and Abebaw, M (2002) *Refugees and Asylum Seekers in the Learning and Skills Council London North Area*, London: LSC London North

UNHCR (2009) *Asylum levels and trends in industrialised countries*, Geneva: UNHCR

Walters N and Egan E, (1996) *Refugee Skills Analysis Report for North West London Training and Enterprise Council*, University of Surrey

Wilson, W (1998) *When work disappears: new implications for race and urban poverty in the Global Economy*. CASE paper 17, London: LSE

Wheatley Price, S (2001) The employment adjustment of male immigrants in England in *Journal of Population Economics*, Vol. 14, pp192-220

Zetter, R, Griffith, D and Sigonda, N (2002) *A survey of policy and practice related to refugee integration*, Brussels: EU

Zetter, R and Pearl, M (2000) The minority within the minority: refugee community-based organisations in the UK and the impact of restrictionalism on asylum seekers. *Journal of Ethnic and Migration Studies* 26 no 4: pp675-697

6

Belonging to the Nation: a comparative study of Somali refugee and asylum seekers living in the UK and Denmark

Gill Valentine, Deborah Sporton
and Katrine Bang Nielsen

The twin forces of the global economy and global conflicts have acce-lerated patterns of transnational migration today, raising questions about how this mobility might shape migrants' sense of belonging and their integration into the societies in which they settle. This chapter provides a comparative study of the integration experiences of Somali refugee and asylum seeker children aged 11 to 18 now living in Sheffield, UK and Aarhus, Denmark. By exploring how young people negotiate and experience their identities in two national contexts with differing integration policy frame-works, we can understand the relationship between integration and identities reveal more about the unintended effects of integration policy on refugee and asylum seekers' feelings of national belonging and identification.

Following the outbreak of civil war in Somalia in 1991, both the UK and Den-mark received substantial numbers of Somali refugees seeking safety in Europe. By 1992 the UN estimated that one million Somalis out of a total population of between five to eleven million were refugees: they were scat-tered in Kenya, Ethiopia, Western Europe, North America and Australasia (Berns McGowan, 1999). As a colonial ruler, the UK has been closely con-nected to Somalia, so there has been a long tradition of Somalis settling in the country.

Somali migration to the UK can be divided into phases. Early in the twentieth century Somali seamen came to work in the British Merchant Navy. When this was run down in the 1950s, Somalis moved to work in the industrial cities of Birmingham, Sheffield and Manchester (Kleist, 2003) and many of the seamen were joined by their families. From the late 1980s onwards, significant numbers of Somalis arrived in the UK seeking refuge from the civil war. The last phase of migration began around 2000, when Somalis who had obtained refugee status and later citizenship in other European countries such as the Netherlands and Denmark began secondary migrations to the UK.

Compared to the long tradition of Somalis living in the UK, Somali migration to Denmark is relatively recent. Most of those living there arrived as asylum seekers fleeing the civil war between the late 1980s and the 1990s (Kleist, 2007). Many obtained refugee status and have subsequently applied for, and received, Danish citizenship. For some Somalis a European passport has given them the opportunity to move on to other western countries, in some cases to reunite with family members (Nielsen, 2004). Recent years have seen a significant number of Somali families leaving Denmark. Given the nature of the diaspora, there are close links between Somalis living in Sheffield and in Aarhus. This close contact came out in the recruitment of research participants. Some Somali families in Sheffield have either lived in Aarhus themselves before undertaking a secondary migration to UK, or have extended family members currently living in Aarhus.

The numbers of Somalis in UK and Denmark are difficult to estimate because of the complex histories of forced and voluntary, internal and international migration as well as the limitations of how data is collected and categorised. It is estimated that about 75,000 Somalis live in the UK and about 15,000 in Denmark. About 5,000 Somalis are thought to be living in Sheffield, compared with approximately 4,000 in Aarhus.

The research used the same methods and research questions in each location. The fieldwork in both was conducted by a researcher who is bilingual in English and Danish and has an intimate knowledge of both societies, languages and cultures, as well as experience of working with the Somali community in both cities. The study included participant observation in Somali community spaces such as homework clubs, various Somali education and community projects and in-depth interviews with key stakeholders who were representatives from local bodies dealing with asylum issues, about the broader contextual issues that shape young people's everyday lives.

Fifty Somali children and the majority of their parents and guardians were recruited for interview, although some of the children were unaccompanied minors. The interviews explored their individual histories of mobility, sense of attachment and understanding of their own identities. The interviewees were selected to include all major arrival scenarios: labour migrants, refugees, asylum seekers and transnational European migrants and ages ranging from 11 to 18. The interviews were conducted in English, Danish or with a Somali interpreter, at a place of the interviewee's choice (Valentine, 1999).

> In making sense of this empirical material, we draw on narrative theories of identity (Somers, 1994). In outlining a narrative approach to identity: it is through narratives and narrativity that we constitute our social identities...all of us come to be who we are (however ephemeral, multiple and changing) by being located or locating ourselves (usually unconsciously) in social narratives rarely of our own making. (Somers, 1994: 606)

In particular, we seek to understand how young Somalis negotiate and discursively position themselves within hegemonic social narratives that are not of their own making but are racialised and gendered, which define what it means to be: British or Danish. Such hegemonic social narratives are powerful in making certain subject positions available to be inhabited, even though the actuality of social categories are more contradictory, fragmented, shifting and ambivalent than dominant public definitions of them (Frosh *et al*, 2002).

At the same time, drawing on the work of Giddens (1991) and Beck (1992), we are alert to how Somali young people produce their own narratives of the self and the particular interpretative repertoires they draw on within this process. We recognise that individuals' identities are never produced along one axis of difference but are intersectional, even though at particular historical moments some social divisions may be more important than others in defining individuals' specific positionings. This involves consideration of how individuals claim some available narratives of identity or disavow others (Valentine, 2007; Valentine and Sporton, 2009). In other words, we follow Brah *et al* (1999:4) in understanding young people's identities to be 'a set of narratives of self-production that are dispersed through a multiplicity of power relations'.

These practices do not occur in a vacuum. We understand identities to be situated accomplishments in that they are enacted in and through different spaces such that one identity category may be used to differentiate another in specific spatial contexts and particular subject positions may become salient or irrelevant in particular spaces (Valentine, 2007; Valentine and Sporton, 2009). Although as individuals our identities might be multiple and fluid, power operates in and through the spaces within which we live and move in systematic ways. One consequence of this is that a given identity is not just something that can be claimed by an individual: it is also dependent, at least in part, on an individual's identity being recognised or accepted by a wider community of practice (Bell *et al*, 1994; Valentine and Skelton, 2007).

A further implication is that performing a given identity in different contexts can define individuals as 'in place' or 'out of place'; as belonging or excluded according to specific spatial norms and expectations (Cresswell, 1996). Here, for example, speaking Somali in a British classroom where the expectation is that only English should be spoken can define a young person as 'out of place'. Speaking Somali in the different spatial context of the local community centre, where the norm is to speak Somali, can be read as a marker of belonging (Valentine *et al*, 2008).

Being Danish, being British: belonging to the nation

The imagining of a national community, while fostering a sense of sameness also necessarily involves delineating boundaries to define who stands outside the nation. Crowley (1999:30) defines the politics of belonging as 'the dirty work of boundary maintenance'. In both Denmark and the UK anxieties about cultural diversification and fears that transnational attachments compromise migrants' allegiance to the host society have resulted in measures to encourage immigrants to develop a greater sense of identification with, and attachment to, the nation state. The responsibility for integration is implicitly seen as the responsibility of immigrants rather than the majority population (Nagel and Staeheli, 2008; Kofman, 2005).

The Somali children interviewed in Aarhus emphasised that they identify as Danish as well as Muslim or Somali. The Danish state places great emphasis on the need for migrants to assimilate, including a policy of dispersing refugees across the country to avoid spatial concentrations in metropolitan areas and to increase refugees' interactions with the majority population (Hamburger, 1990). All newly arrived adult (18+) refugees must take part in a three year 'integration programme', where they are taught about Danish society and culture and to speak the language, and undergo other training to prepare them for the labour market. In order to get permanent status a refugee must complete the integration programme, pass a Danish language test and a test about Danish society and have no convictions or debts. When refugee children start school in Denmark they are sent to 'reception classes' in specific schools where they are taught Danish intensively, alongside other subjects, so as to prepare them for entry into a mainstream classroom. Increasingly, new initiatives to provide kindergarten places for refugee children are being introduced to ensure that they are able to speak Danish before they reach school age.

Many of the Somali families living in Aarhus speak Danish in the family home as well as in public spaces. This differs from Sheffield Somalis, who mostly speak Somali at home. Some of the young people interviewed explained that they speak Danish better than they do Somali. This is significant because language is an important marker of identity: you are what you speak, and what you speak is where you are (Valentine *et al*, 2008). Spatial norms influence the languages that children chose to speak and speaking a given language has an affect, it makes people feel a sense of identity and belonging and shapes how they talk about their lives. A 13 year old boy describes the role of the Danish language to his self-identity thus:

> I have been here most of my life and I have been going to a Danish school, have Danish friends and speak Danish most of the time. So Danish has a lot to do with who I am.

Yet despite enacting a Danish identity through language, many of the Somali young people interviewed in Aarhus described encountering significant experiences of discrimination in everyday life (cf Essed, 1991). While Danish society has traditionally imagined itself to be a liberal and tolerant place, predicated on a strong commitment to social equality in the context of a supportive welfare state, social attitudes have shifted in reaction to the perceived threats of European integration and associated immigration (Wren, 2001). Since the early 1990s there has been growing concern within Denmark about immigration and integration, which has seen a tightening of asylum legislation, an increased focus on the importance of preserving Danish culture, and immigrants have been discouraged from maintaining transnational relations with their diasporic communities. There has also been the emergence of far-right groups (Hjarnø, 1991; Østergaard-Nielsen, 2002). Immigrants are often referred to in popular discourse as 'the strangers', suggesting that they are not seen as belonging in the national imagination. Research has identified evidence of widespread discrimination in housing policies and the compulsory dispersal of refugees, practices which have scarcely faced opposition from the liberal professional establishment (Wren, 1999). A mother described some of the racist and Islamaphobic prejudices that Somalis encounter in Denmark:

> I think that many immigrants have problems when they live in Denmark. There are a lot of negative things being communicated in the media. It's very difficult being an immigrant and I think it's very difficult getting into the Danish system

> ... You can communicate if you speak the language but the system, it's very difficult ... The labour market distinguishes between Danes and immigrants and they say: 'Aha, he's not a Jensen or Hansen. He's called something else such as Mohammed'. And then there are other problems arising ... Once I applied for a job and then the employer asked me 'You are Muslim and I'm Christian, how can we work together?' (mother, Aarhus)

According to some commentators, the reception of Somalis in Denmark has been negative compared with the response to other war refugees such as Bosnians. The media and politicians frequently focus on problems of integration, and target Somalis for special measures such as repatriation (Fink-Nielsen *et al*, 2004; Fadel *et al*, 1999). This phenomenon in Danish society has been described by some as 'Somaliphobia', embracing, as it does, both racism and Islamaphobia. It has provoked Somali representatives to complain to the United Nations High Commissioner for Refugees and to request that refugees be located in a more tolerant country (Fadel *et al*, 1999; Nielsen, 2004a; *Dansk Flygtningehjælp*, 1998). Perhaps unsurprisingly, a desire to escape such prejudice and discrimination is one of the most common reasons for Somalis to undertake secondary migration from Denmark to the UK. Indeed, Hamburger (1990) has argued that although the aim of Danish policy has been to integrate migrants into Danish society, the effect has been to legitimate negative attitudes by the white majority secular population towards migrants and their culture. This girl explains how the intersection of her race and faith define her as a stranger in Denmark despite her self-identity as Danish, making her want to live in Somalia where she feels she will belong, even though she speaks Danish more fluently than Somali:

> Aziza: [at school] everyone talked in Danish even the Somalis...I'm used to speaking Danish. That's my language. I speak Danish better than I speak Somali. I like it ... I would like to see my own country [Somalia]. Here [in Denmark] I'm a stranger ... I would like to live in my own country and to get used to speaking my own language and live according to my culture [Edit].
>
> Interviewer: You said that you feel like a stranger here?
>
> Aziza: Yes, my skin colour and my religion, these two things, they [Danes] notice and then I feel a stranger ... I get really sad when personally you feel that you are [Danish] and other people don't feel that. Then you feel really bad, when somebody says 'Go back to your own country' it really hurts (girl aged 14 Aarhus).

Thus while the Danish policy of integration aims to encourage migrants to become Danish by inculcating them into a shared language and common culture so re-shaping what it means to be Somali and how this should be enacted in practice, many of our Somali respondents do not feel at home in Danish society because they do not feel safe: belonging and integration is not just about being able to fit in, it is fundamentally about emotional attachment and security (Yuval Davis, 2006). The Somali respondents in Aarhus identify as Danish because they can competently enact a Danish identity by speaking Danish, dressing in a European style, and having the cultural knowledge to participate in Danish society but they still do not feel they belong to the nation because they are black and Muslim. It is this intersection of their race and faith identities which defines them as outside the nation.

In the UK there has also been growing public debate about immigration and the gradual tightening of the asylum system since the late 1990s, such as the Immigration and Asylum Act of 1999. However, until 2006, when the UK Government changed the regulations regarding the acquisition of citizenship, establishing learning English as a formal requirement for attaining citizenship and introducing a citizenship test, ceremonies and oaths, British governments had been much less prescriptive (Kymlicka, 2003) than Danish governments in defining prerequisites for citizenship. This perhaps reflects the UK's colonial history, which has made the issue of naturalisation and loyalty more sensitive, and the complex patterns of immigration into the UK throughout the 20th century.

Kymlicka (2003) argues that it was always difficult to suggest that immigrants to the UK needed re-socialising into British culture, given that many had been raised in societies whose legal, political and education were designed by British imperial masters. While anti-immigration rhetoric did permeate the Conservative government of the 1980s and has a lineage dating back to debates about post-war commonwealth migration to the UK in the 1960s, there had been little explicit policy emphasis on 'integration'. But this is now emerging more strongly in contemporary political discourse (Kofman, 2005; Nagel and Staeheli, 2008). In the context of a loose policy of multiculturalism, migrants, despite racist rhetoric and well-documented discrimination, have had relative freedom to define their own identities and to create their own communities. There are also a number of public bodies such as the Equality and Human Rights Commission and other liberal-professional bodies oriented towards anti-racism that have sought to advance the rights of minority ethnic groups and inform these communities of their entitlements.

This form of support and protection has until recently been absent in Denmark (Wren, 2001).

There is a strong, well-established Somali community in Sheffield, although it is fractured by clan allegiances and other differences. Most of the young people we interviewed identify first and foremost as Muslim and Somali, with many disavowing British identity, unlike the Aarhus Somalis' claims to be Danish despite their experiences of exclusion.

In Sheffield the Somali language is regarded by parents as an important vehicle through which children learn to be Somali, and as crucial if their children are to be able to communicate with, and therefore have a sense of belonging, to families whose members might be scattered across the diaspora. For many of the parents the possibility of a return, a visit or a permanent homecoming to Somalia figures significantly in their geographical imaginations (Valentine *et al,* 2008). Accordingly, ensuring that their children are fluent in Somali is paryt of the preparation for their imagined futures. Here, a mother describes the importance she places on speaking Somali at home if her children are to retain a Somali and familial identity despite living in Sheffield.

> Because still my Mum and my Dad, they live in Somalia and also all my other relatives they live in Somalia, so I'm thinking maybe one day they [the children] meet them ... it's hard and embarrassing if someone, you know, they give the translation to your own Grandma [laughs] when you are speaking. So ... I teach them at least to speak the Somali. (mother, Sheffield)

Sheffield Somalis are critical of secondary migrants arriving from Europe for not teaching their children the Somali language – in the same way that they lament their lax interpretations of what it means to be Muslim – and for therefore not being proper 'Somalis'. In such ways, the Sheffield Somalis are producing their own narratives of identities in opposition to assimilation narratives:

> Well it's, I mean compared to, most Somali people like, they've lived either in Holland or in Denmark or just other places and they act like the people would down there [sic] and compared to the Somali people that children that just like came from Somalia, we don't act the same. And most of the time we don't really understand each other. (girl, 15, Sheffield)

While many of the Somalis interviewed in Sheffield have more freedom to enact Muslim and Somali identities through embodied performances such as dress, bodily comportment and language, and have disavowed the identity of

British, they nonetheless described feeling safe and at home in the UK. Across the Somali diaspora there is an image of Britain as a place of freedom to be whoever you are (Nielsen, 2004). This image is expressed by some of the Somali families in Sheffield who have lived in other European countries. One Somali woman who migrated from Denmark to the UK describes life in Sheffield in the following way:

> I feel that I live in my country, like in Somalia. Because my cousins, my aunts, my uncles, they live here [in Sheffield]. And it's so free, I feel so free ... [In Denmark] all the time on the television they talked about refugees and Somalis. Oh, it's difficult to relax then ... There's a big difference between Denmark and the UK. If we talk about Sheffield, there are many Somalis. So when we lived in Denmark, my children spoke Danish fluently and only a little Somali. But now they speak Somali fluently [laughs] because so many Somalis live here, and they play together with them, and the neighbours are Somali, and they go to school with Somalis, so they speak a lot of Somali ... So when people speak Somali here when you go outside, you think that you're in Somalia. I'm happy about this. (mother, Sheffield)

Although some Sheffield interviewees did describe experiencing racism, these negative events are countered by a broader perception of finding safety and trust that comes from being part of a strong and stable local Somali Muslim community. There are parallels with Phillips *et al*'s (2007) study of British Asian residential choices, which found that the respondents valued living in 'segregated communities' because there they were free from racial harassment and obtained community support. It might also reflect the fact that in spite of racism and xenophobia in Britain (Hewitt, 2005) there has also been another more benevolent history in the UK of hospitality: what Nava (2006) describes in relation to London as a 'domestic cosmopolitanism'. Amin (2003), too, observes that mainstream British society has become more cosmopolitan and tolerant since he arrived in the UK 30 years ago. He attributes this change in part to a public culture which, following the election of a Labour government in 1997, has addressed institutional racism, discrimination and racially motivated violence, as well as the importance of the micropolitics of everyday social encounters in overcoming cultural differences. In one sense then, Somalis in Sheffield feel that they belong in the UK because they are secure in their local community, without necessarily being included in, or self-identifying with, the nation.

Conclusion

This chapter has shown that belonging to a nation is not just about citizenship *per se* and having rights and responsibilities; it is about 'the emotions that such memberships evoke' (Yuval-Davis *et al*, 2005:526). Specifically, it is about the security that being in 'place' provides. The Aarhus Somalis do not feel that they belong. Even though they enact a Danish identity through language and dress, they remain 'strangers' without a liveable place within the nation. Their networks and ability to reproduce a community of practice are fragile and precarious, leaving them feeling vulnerable to prejudice and discrimination in the face of narrow definitions of Danish nationhood which are predicated on secularism and whiteness. In contrast, the Sheffield Somalis feel that they belong in the UK – even though they do not identify as British – because at local level they have defined their own community in terms of shared values, networks and practices, and in this way have made the place their own. So they feel secure within their community and feel that they have a stake in its future.

This stability and emotional sense of being part of a larger whole, which resonates from a sense of having a place to be, affords the Sheffield Somalis the freedom to define their own narratives of identity predicated on the complex intersection of race, faith and gender identities beyond narrow prescriptions of Britishness. For the Sheffield Somalis, integration is about a commitment to the place-based community where they live; it does not require them to adopt the cultural membership of Britishness, nor does it require them to deny their transnational affiliations. In this way their sense of integration and belonging in the UK is built, paradoxically, not out of an attachment to the nation but from complex webs of emotion and identification which include the complex intersection of race, faith and gender that span local and transnational scales.

This comparison of the experiences of Somalis living in Aarhus and Sheffield has potential UK policy implications in the light of the recent Interim Statement produced by the Commission on Integration and Cohesion (2007). This contained a warning that by promoting respect for difference, UK policy may be facilitating separation rather than integration. It identified 'Britishness' as an important potential unifying force, although Britishness was not defined. And it argued that an inability to speak English is a critical barrier to the integration of migrant groups and to cohesion. This was followed shortly afterwards (February, 2007) by an announcement from the Department of Work and Pensions that learning to speak English might soon become a prerequisite for receiving welfare benefits in the UK. In many respects this rhetoric about the importance of speaking English and the promotion of ill-defined notions of Britishness bear echoes of the Danish policy of integration.

However, as the evidence from Aarhus suggests, the danger is that such attempts to reduce or stabilise migrants' identities into narrow categories of belonging will threaten the space to define their own narratives of identity. Yet it is the very possibility to achieve integration by participating in the places where they live without having to deny their transnational affiliations as Somali and as Muslim which gives migrant groups, such as Somalis in Sheffield, the security to feel they belong. At the same time, ill-defined notions of Britishness also risk legitimising negative attitudes by the majority population towards migrants and their cultures rather than promoting its responsibility for fostering integration by recognising the presence of minorities, and need to respect and accommodate their needs. In this respect the Interim Statement produced by the Commission on Integration and Cohesion (2007: 33) is on to something when it states: 'Integration and cohesion will always be about place'.

Acknowledgments

We wish to acknowledge the support of the ESRC (RES-148-25-0028) for funding the research on which this paper is based. We are grateful to all the children, parents and key stakeholders who gave up their time to share their experiences and opinions with us. Elements of this chapter have been taken from an article (Valentine Sporton, 2009) previously published in *Environment and Planning D: society and space*. We are grateful to the publishers for permission to republish it here.

Note

1 Quotations from the interview used in this article are verbatim. Spoken or grammatical errors have not been corrected. Interviews conducted in Danish or with a Somali interpreter have been translated into English – with some inevitable loss of meaning (Smith, 1996)

References

Amin, A (2003) Unruly strangers? The 2001 urban riots in Britain. *International Journal of Urban and Regional Research* 27 pp460-63

Anthias, F (2006) Belongings in a globalising and unequal world: rethinking translocations. In N Yuval-Davis, K Kannabiran UM Vieten (ed) *The Situated Politics of Belonging*, London: Sage

Beck, U (1992) *Risk Society*, London: Sage

Bell, D, Binnie, J, Cream, J. and Valentine, G (1994) All hyped up and no place to go. *Gender, Place and Culture* 1 pp31-47

Berns McGowan, R (1999) *Muslims in the Diaspora: the Somali communities of London and Toronto*, Toronto: University of Toronto Press

Brah, A, Hickman, MJ and Mac an Ghaill, M (1999) Thinking Identities: Ethnicity, Racism and Culture in A Brah, MJ Hickman, and M Mac an Ghaill (eds) *Thinking Identities: ethnicity, racism and culture*, Basingstoke: Macmillan

Commission on Integration and Cohesion (2007) *Our Interim Statement.* www.integrationand cohesion.org.uk. Accessed 23 February 2007

Cresswell, T (1996) *In Place/Out of Place: geography, ideology and transgression*, Minneapolis, MN: University of Minnesota Press

Crowley, J (1999) The politics of belonging: some theoretical considerations, in A Geddes and A, Favell (eds) *The Politics of Belonging: migrants and minorities in contemporary Europe*, Aldershot: Ashgate.

Danish Refugee Council (2004) *Flygtninge i Danmark – Integration,* København: Danish Refugee Council.

Dansk Flygtningehjælp (1998) Integration *Nyhedsbrev.* May

Dwyer, C (1999) Veiled meanings: young British Muslim women and the negotiation of difference, *Gender, Place and Culture* 6 pp5-26

Dwyer, C (2000) Negotiating diasporic identities: young British South Asian Muslim women. *Women's Studies International Forum* 23 pp475-486

Essed, P (1991) *Understanding Everyday Racism: an interdisciplinary theory,* London: Sage

EUMC (2006) *Annual Report on the Situation Regarding Racism and Xenophobia in the Member States of the EU.* Vienna: The European Monitoring Centre on Racism and Xenophobia

Fadel, U (1999) *De 'besværlige' somaliere.* In P Hervik (ed) *Den Generende Forskellighed – Danske svar på den stigende multikulturalisme* København: Hans Reitzels Forlag

Fink-Nielsen, M, Hansen, P and Kleist, N (2004) Roots, rights and responsibilities, place-making and repatriation among Somalis in Denmark and Somaliland. *Vienna Journal of Critical Affairs*

Frosh, S, Phoenix, A, and Pattman, R (2002) *Young Masculinities: understanding boys in contemporary society,* Basingstoke: Palgrave

Giddens, A (1991) *Modernity and Self-Identity: self and society in late modern age*, Cambridge: Polity Press

Griffiths, D (2002) *Somali and Kurdish Refugees in London: new identities in the diaspora*, London: Ashgate,

Hamburger, C (1990) Assimilation som grundtræk i dansk indvandrerpolitik. *Politica* 22

Haverluck, T (1998) Hispanic community types and assimilation in Mex-America, *Professional Geographer* 50 pp465-480

Hewitt, R (2005) *White Backlash and the Politics of Multiculturalism*, Cambridge: Cambridge University Press

Hjarnø, J (1991) Migrants and refugees on the Danish labour market. *New Community* 18 pp75-87

Kleist, N (2003) Nomads, sailors and refugees: a century of Somali migration. *Sussex Migration, Working Paper* 23, Brighton: University of Sussex

Kleist, N (2007) Ambivalent Encounters. Negotiating boundaries of Danishness, Somaliness, and belonging. in A M Kusow and S Bjørk (eds) *From Mogadishu to Dixon., The Somali diaspora in a global perspective.* Lawrenceville, NJ: Africa World Press/Red Sea Press

Kofman, E (2005) Citizenship, migration and the re-assertion of national identity, *Citizenship Studies* 9 pp453-467

Kymlicka, W (2003) Immigration, citizenship, multiculturalism: exploring the links. *The Political Quarterly* p195-208

Massey, D and Jess, P (1995) Places and cultures in an uneven world, in D Massey and P Jess (eds) *A Place in the World? Places, cultures and globalization*, Milton Keynes: Open University Press

Nagel, CR, and Staeheli, LA (2008) Integration and the negotiation of 'here' and 'there': the case of British Arab activists, *Social and Cultural Geography* 9 pp415-430

Nava, M (2006) Domestic cosmopolitanism and structures of feeling: the specificity of London, in N Yuval-Davis, K Kannabiran and UM Vieten (eds) *The Situated Politics of Belonging*. London: Sage

Nielsen, K B (2004) Next stop Britain: The influence of transnational networks on the secondary movement of Danish Somalis. *Sussex Migration Working Paper* No. 22 Brighton: University of Sussex

Østergaard-Nielsen, E (2002) *Politik over Grænser. tyrkere og kurderes engagement i det politiske liv i hjemlandet,* Aarhus: Magtudredningen

Phillips, D, Davis, C and Ratcliffe, C (2007) British Asian narratives of urban space. *Transactions of the Institute of British Geographers* 32 pp217-234

Smith, FM (1996) Problematising language: limitations and possibilities in 'foreign language' research, *Area* 28 pp160-166

Somers, MR (1994) The narrative constitution of identity: a relational and network approach, *Theory and Society* 23 pp605-649

Valentine, G (1999) Being seen and heard? Ethical dilemmas of research with children and young people. *Journal of Ethics, Place and Environment* 2 pp141—155

Valentine, G (2007) Theorising and researching intersectionality: a challenge for feminist geography, *The Professional Geographer* 59 pp10-21

Valentine, G and Skelton, TL (2007) Redefining 'norms': D/deaf young people's transitions to independence, *Sociological Review* 55 pp104-123

Valentine, G, and Sporton, D (2009) 'How other people see you, it's like nothing that's inside': the impact of processes of disidentification and disavowal on young people's subjectivities, *Sociology,* 43 (4) pp737-753.

Valentine, G, Sporton, D and Bang Nielsen, K (2008) Language use on the move: sites of encounter, identities and belonging. *Transactions of the Institute of British Geographers* 33 pp376-387.

Valentine, G, Sporton, D, and Bang Nielsen, K (2009) Identities and belonging: a study of Somali refugee and asylum seekers living in the UK and Denmark, *Environment and Planning D: society and space*, 27(2) 234 – 250

Wren, K (1999) International Migration to Denmark: Majority and Minority Perspectives, Unpublished Ph.D. thesis available from Department of Geography, University of Dundee.

Wren, K (2001) Cultural racism: something rotten in the state of Denmark? *Social and Cultural Geography* 2 pp141-22.

Yuval-Davis, N (2006) Belonging and the politics of belonging, *Patterns of Prejudice* 40 pp196-212.

Yuval-Davis, N, Anthias, F and Kofman, E (2005) Secure borders and safe haven and the gendered politics of belonging, *Ethnic and Racial Studies* 28 pp513-535

7

'Until yesterday we lived together *Do juce smo zivjeli zajedno*': Youth and community development in Northern Ireland and Bosnia-Herzegovina

Alan Grattan, Marina Zhunich and Martin McMullan

Introduction

In the contemporary runaway world, few societies, communities or individuals escape the globalising effect that impacts upon our everyday lives; each society finds itself in the midst of either gradual or eruptive political, social and economic change. Reflexive modernisation is often a product of this process, which creates societal and communal uncertainty following the decline or erosion of institutional and cultural certainties. This feeling of insecurity tends to be further intensified in the communities emerging from the experience of prolonged violent conflict, such as Northern Ireland (NI) and Bosnia-Herzegovina (BaH). In these societies communal segregation and separation is regarded as normal and essential for both physical security and survival of identity. Such a situation serves to further reinforce distrust, prejudice, suspicion and hatred of the 'other'.

The change creates mass social and psychological issues that need to be addressed on a communal and individual level. Often the negative social response is one of counter modernisation, based upon a dynamic interplay of tradition, nationalism, ethnocentrism, xenophobia and violence. For many communities the certainties of the past are replaced by the perceived uncertainties of the future. And often it is the young people in these situations who find themselves the primary victims, caught between the past and present and striving to make their future. The consequences of localised segregation and the demands of dealing with globalised notions of integration add pressure and provoke feelings of existential anxiety.

In the realm of civil society, youth and community development work must engage not only with the local community, history and tradition but also with the influence of modern globalism and consumerism, to gain the hearts and minds of young people. Drawing on initiatives and experiences from both BaH and NI, this chapter highlight some positive practice as well as some of the barriers encountered in relation to youth and community development and social cohesion.

Northern Ireland and Bosnia-Herzegovina: the common theoretical context

Following years of conflict NI and BaH find themselves in a prolonged period of rebuilding and restructuring. While the level of intensity and nature of their respective conflicts may be different the net result was very similar; violence, death, destruction and displacement. Whereas NI found itself in a 35 year protracted conflict over the destiny of the country, BaH became embroiled in a war that was to last for three bloody and violent years. The similarities stem from the fact that both conflicts emanated from cultural, ethnic and religious division and that both were to determine the future destiny and identity of the country (Poulton, 1994; di Giovanni, 2005; Malcolm, 1996; McKitterick and McVea, 2001; Bowyer Bell, 1993; Coogan, 1995).

Another common element is that both conflicts involved an internal struggle between communities who inhabited the same land but held different national, political and cultural aspirations. Until the eruption of conflict the communities in BaH and NI did show tolerance and a degree of understanding towards their respective neighbours; an uneasy co-existence prevailed, encapsulated by the title: *Until Yesterday We Lived Together – Do juce smo zivjeli zajedno*. In both conflicts young people were of central significance as both victims and perpetrators of violence (Gallagher, 2004; Hamilton *et al*, 2004; Hanson, 2005; Muldoon, 2004; Reilly *et al*, 2004).

The advent of their conflicts shattered the uneasy co-existence. Communities were driven apart by prejudice, discrimination, hatred, violence and killing. Within both societies, communities became totally divided and segregated. This led to the emergence of self-contained and separated civil societies, co-existing in isolation from one another within the single geo-political state. In both NI and BaH isolation, separation, segregation and communal division became the accepted order, both during and after the conflict.

Both societies are subject to processes of the external and fast changing world in which they must exist and develop; changes at global level impact upon the local. This particularly applies when societies and communities are emerging from the experiences of war and conflict. McGhee (2005:5) asserts 'in the midst and aftermath of this process there is often at one level or another, an attempt to re-establish or recreate a sense of order and stability', while Grattan (2007b:63) adds, 'in a fast changing world, increasingly individuals and communities search for a sense of security in an insecure world'. Often this is sought by recourse to their history and traditions that are seen to be under threat by the 'common ideological framework' espoused by global forces (Conteh-Morgan, 2001:4).

A further dimension of the search for security is the holding on to a sense of community as a 'protective shell' (Sennett, 1974).This is based upon an increased sense of existential anxiety at both the individual and communal level; a reaffirmation of self-identity is crucial. Grattan (2007b:63-64) continues,

> the sense that one's long standing perceived identity and traditions are being questioned or changed in the modern era adds to the heightened sense of existential anxiety and the attraction of looking to one's past for security.

Counter-modernisation in this context is seen as an act of social defence that is infused with emotion; community, tradition, culture and identity are to be defended at all costs.

When this occurs there tends to be a negative response against the processes of modernisation. At a localised, day to day lived reality, responses to the encroachment and threat of the outside and globalising forces is often personalised, internalised and directed negatively towards the 'other' (Grattan, 2007b:68). In the case of BaH and NI, the 'other' is still very much the traditional or historical adversary, the 'other' community. Despite the cessation of violence, tensions between the respective communities remain alive in their respective world views.

In this context reflexive modernisation is deemed to refer to 'conscious deliberations that take place through 'internal conversations' ... the basis upon which [people] determine their future course of action' (Archer, 2007:3-4). However, an uneasy co-existence often develops between reflexive modernisation and negative social responses based on nationalism, xenophobia, ethno-

centrism and violence. Sennett (1974) argues that one of the central characteristics of such responses by a society or community is often based upon
emotion. In this respect Mabel Berezin (2002) refers to a 'community of feelings' as a mechanism that moulds together emotions, community and action.
A frequent consequence of this reversion to the community as a means of
creating a defensive and reassuring environment is the development of an
insular and backward-looking attitude. People became unwilling to enter
into dialogue, discussion or processes of reconciliation with the perceived
'other'. Grattan (2007a:53) argues that in such a situation visible and invisible
barriers are created by a community and its individual members; both have
emotionally withdrawn from the world and have erected a territorial, symbolic and psychological barrier to keep the world out. For Sennett, community becomes the 'territory of 'warm' feeling versus the territory of im-
personal blankness' (1974:300).

In such circumstances, even after the violence has subsided, social and communal segregation can and often does intensify, producing a stand-off
attitude that further entrenches emotions and divisions; mutual suspicion,
distrust and myth increasingly become part of community reality. In this
segregated situation moral outrage is utilised as a means of galvanising
individuals into a solidarity on each side of the divide. Sennett observes that
internal passion and external withdrawal must be maintained through the
'hyping up of emotions' by recourse to culture and tradition (1974:307). The
creation of the visible and invisible barriers is made all the easier within an
increasingly segregated society and legitimises actions and attitudes that
keep the 'other' at a safe distance. Suspicion, distrust, fear and hatred only reinforce the position of those who remain dogmatic and uncompromising. For
such communities 'distrust and solidarity seemingly opposed are united'
(Sennett, 1974:309).

Add to this the increasing alienation of youth from society and the absence of
any meaningful political and communal participation and then perhaps
youth apathy becomes inevitable. One of the main challenges of youth work
is to engage in those communities where the challenge is to capture the
hearts and minds of young people. Often this will bring youth work into direct
ideological confrontation with community leaders who favour a direct and
uncompromising approach to the defence of the community against the con-
taminating outside world or the 'other' communities (Grattan and Morgan,
2007:165-175).

Youth workers must engage in a real and meaningful way with how young people make sense of their world, society and community, as well as their emotions of fear, anger and hatred that may lead to anti-social activities, conflict or even violence. They must learn to listen and encourage young people to learn to listen to their internal conversations and recognise that any actions that may arise from these thoughts will carry consequences: they are deeply infused with both positive and negative emotions.

Programmes and policies for cultural and political expression must be encouraged – not simply youth forums and parliaments but community based initiatives that address the real issues that impact upon that community and its youth. Also, youth work in its philosophy, policy making, training and practice must become more radicalised and prepared to address both local and global political issues. The global affects the local at individual and community level: youth work must address social division and segregation and its consequences for young people, whether that society is in a process of divergence – moving towards conflict – or of convergence – in the process of reconstruction and reconciliation (Grattan and Morgan, 2007). In both situations youth and community development work has a crucial and significant contribution to make.

The following are some of the experiences and examples of work undertaken with young people in the communities of BaH and NI, where both societies, years after the cessation of conflict, still remain deeply divided and segregated at community level.

The Youth and Community Context: the experience of Youth Action Northern Ireland (YANI)

YANI are keen to readdress the importance of community relations and the role of those working with young people to enhance a stable and civic society and have an extensive range of cross-community programmes located across NI. They also believe that engaging the most marginalised young people is the challenge facing a lasting peace. Two of YANI's key objectives are to:

- provide opportunities for young people in communities to contribute to the peace building process
- support a legacy of young leaders with the skills and confidence to move communities beyond conflict and contribute to solutions for lasting peace

The 'Making it r wrld 2' (YANI, 2004:16) consultation on a strategy for children and young people in NI indicates that, although Northern Ireland is emerging from conflict, it is still a deeply divided society; children as young as three or four years old have been found to identify with their own side and by ten and eleven years old are expressing fear and antagonism toward the other side. In supporting young people to build a shared and peaceful society YANI values their potential and works with them and with their workers to consider effective ways of addressing segregation and sectarianism. The agency has over thirty years experience in community relations work and feels a responsibility to respond to the violence and conflict surrounding young people as they grew up.

Accordingly, the organisation developed innovative cross-community, political education and community relations programmes with young people from a range of backgrounds throughout the 1980s and 1990s. Training for youth workers was piloted, refined and accredited, assisting youth workers and associated professionals to build skills in delivering community relations programmes, conflict resolution and mediation. As well as the development of community relations publications, YANI has more recently been delivering the accredited 'Introduction to Community Relations and Equity, Diversity and Interdependence Work with Young People' course based on core principles of community relations work and exploring NI as an increasingly multicultural and pluralist society.

YANI initiated the Newry and Armagh Area Based Youth Work Strategy (NI), located in the south eastern part of Northern Ireland and the border with the Republic of Ireland. The area comprises two urban centres and a large rural population. The three year initiative (2004-2006) was designed to develop co-ordination in enhancing services and opportunities for young people in contributing to a peaceful society. It involved a comprehensive needs assessment and resulted in the report by McMullan, McShane and Grattan, (2006) *It's always in the back of your mind.*

The Newry and Armagh report presents a picture of the lives of young people within the area, with the report title coming from one of the young people involved in the research. The quote implies that even though the hostilities may be receding there are still lingering prejudices, fears and suspicions. In relation to the everyday lives of young people, *It's always in the back of your mind* encapsulates the conscious thoughts that affect young people's choices, behaviours and attitudes. This can mean being afraid of the areas in which they socialise, work or hang out, as Newry and Armagh have been badly affected by the realities of the conflict. A legacy of the conflict is the many polarised communities with territory marked out by flags and emblems. This was particularly the case in Newry and Armagh, where local populations had been displaced from their original hinterlands. Polarisation of communities, lack of opportunities and emigration of young people have been ongoing issues in this area.

Young people are particularly affected by isolation and marginalisation: most of them grow up, attend school and socialise within their own communities. In the rural areas of Newry and Armagh these effects are compounded by the lack of transport and the geographical isolation. The young people feel excluded from active participation in community life: many do not venture outside the area they live in, causing even further polarisation.

Sectarianism has been identified by young people as a key issue, one that manifests itself in fighting after school. Their school uniforms are a means of identification of their religion and cultural identity and they can subject one another to physical and mental abuse. Consequently many young people avoid Armagh city centre, thereby reinforcing segregation.

The findings of the YANI report (2006) reinforced those of Hargie *et al*, (1998: 7), who found that young people were affected by what they called the 'bubble syndrome': they felt comfortable and secure in the micro society of their own community and did not wish to leave the protective bubble. Many of the respondents in both studies referred to the 'bubble syndrome', in relation to their reluctance to work outside their own immediate area. This syndrome creates fear of going to a different area, and makes them consciously decide to stay within their carefully defined zone of comfort and safety. This establishes a mindset of insularity and reduced horizons.

Even within these protective bubble communities, young people still encounter mixed messages from adults. Their perceptions of violence are often shaped by local history, by parental and community influence, as well as by direct experiences of violence. Despite the peace process, violence remains an immediate memory for many young people and makes them wary of building friendships with young people from another tradition.

Some of these issues were further reinforced by YANI's *Everyday Life* (2001), a report on young men and violence. YANI found that many young men living in NI, having been brought up in a society that used violence as a means of dealing with conflict, often see violence as a means of defending themselves and also their community. Some of their subjects stated that violence was an integral part of their everyday life, and that the fear of potential violence remained with them throughout their lives. The report found that, although most young men have to deal constantly with violence and live in fear in their own communities, the majority had never discussed or reflected on violence or its impact on them. The research further highlighted that peace building needs to proactively extend dialogue between the Catholic and Protestant communities as well as including minority groups.

This has led to calls for the need for initiatives with young people to prepare them for a changing society in which they can embrace difference and share life with others who have different backgrounds to themselves. A central component of peace building is building a legacy in which young people and adults are working together to shape a future which works to eradicate prejudice and discrimination. At an initial baseline however young people continue to feel left out of decision making and as having no real input into strategies and plans that will have an impact on them and their areas. There has to be a level of trust, respect and confidence between adults and young people. This will lead to more effective youth participation and confidence, and a growth in young people's active involvement in peace building.

Without instigating peace building initiatives for young people, the deeply held prejudice, attitudes and behaviours will persist. This is worrying, as young people frequently refer to the impact of violence and aggression on their everyday lives and how difficult it is to avoid it or to deal with situations in a way which does not compromise their identity or status.

Those working with young people need to be trained and supported in developing inclusive practice which requires detailed strategies and plans. It is crucial for educators and youth workers to open up exploration of issues that are sensitive, emotive and political. YANI argue that youth initiatives should proactively address diversity, integration, inclusion and inter-culturalism in supporting young people to prepare for a shared future.

Youth and Community: initiatives in post-conflict Bosnia and Herzegovina (BaH)

The Youth sector in BaH fully reflects, and is a product of, the socio-political hostilities of the nineties. The generation which will be ruling the country in ten years time was either brought up among the brutalities of the war or grew up in exile in the UK, Germany, Austria, the US or Scandinavia. Yet exile, even when forced, is now praised by many young people who had the chance to escape the atrocities of war: they admit that at home they would not have received such good education, language skills or personal experiences.

Some of these nostalgic diaspora youth are now returning to their roots to use their westernised skills. Despite such positive changes, this is not enough to implant western democratic standards into BaH soil. Constant political problems have tended to alienate young people from political institutions and politics in general: the socially insecure situation pushes some of them into what may be deemed to be anti-social choices.

In the main the key issues that are of direct relevance to BaH youth – employment, housing, education, and extra curricula activities – are tackled by local and international NGOs more often than local authorities. Various youth and community development agencies such as the Youth Informative Agency (OIA), the Centre for informative decontamination of youth, Infopart, the Youth group of the Human Rights Centre, the Youth Employment Services, and the Youth Council of the Republic of Srpska all try to address the situation, to set new cultural trends, to stimulate young people to think and to radically change their mindset.

As well as the NGOs, the involvement of the international community is essential, including bodies like the Organisation for Security and Co-operation in Europe (OSCE), UNESCO, and the Council of Europe, which targets the same issues in a different and more systematic way, applying its moral and political authority.

Unfortunately, not all the stakeholders have a strategic view on how to make progress in this delicate youth-in-post-conflict environment. The NGOs which flooded in immediately after the war tended to invest in ambitious one-off projects like reconstruction, civic initiatives, the start up of small and medium enterprises, and female education rather than strategic sustainable future-oriented development initiatives.

The same problem generally applies to youth policies where 16 to 25 year olds who grew up in a war environment are diverted into short-term and sporadic activities. These are characterised by excessive international financial attention, providing trips to Europe and certificates for participation but seldom demand accountability. These young people rarely undergo training which could serve their longer term skills and intellectual development and imbue values that transcend those imposed by their own ethnic group and community. Training is more likely to run counter to global values.

It was crucial to start building the civil society sector immediately after the war. Usually the NGOs were located downtown and would operate inside their area, thereby ignoring suburban and especially rural youth. Since civil society has been established, the focus needs to switch to them. The rural youth policy section needs its own strategy and youth work structures need to be established and subsidised from the municipal budget.

The OSCE promotes an integrated approach to youth as part of the civil society. OSCE has also worked with youth branches of political parties over the last twelve years. Programmes included strategic planning, writing project proposals, team-building seminars, and developing dialogue skills, tolerance and ethics in politics workshops. These were aimed at bringing about a new generation of young ambitious politicians who would share the democratic values advocated by the organisations. However, the international community's ideology could not compete with the strong domestic influence of the main nationalist parties.

Many of the local and international NGOs have opted for confidence building and tolerance seminars as a way to boost democratic awareness in BaH. Normally these projects are held in the form of round tables or creative workshops that allow people to express their frustration and formulate some basic principles of peaceful co-existence. But some of these events, financed with international money and conceived by foreigners who are unaware of local complexities, can deepen the disappointment that some BaH youth feel about civil society. In summer 2007, for example, a US funded NGO promoting peace and dialogue opened a park in Mostar where Bosniak and Croat children could come and play together. The event was widely reported by media but they failed to mention that the park was in a heavily segregated part of the city which would hardly unite the two ethnic groups. Observers argue that any activity to animate often apathetic and disappointed youth is better than none – but careful thought could generate more effective initiatives.

The overall effect of the various democratic programmes, however, has made a number of active, passionate and knowledgeable young people ready to hold sustainable dialogue with authorities. They have the skills to build relationships with foreign donors and are aware of their rights and their freedom to make choices. Although still a minority, these young people might well become the catalyst for future changes.

Concluding comments

NI, like BaH, has experienced just over a decade of relative peace and both are engaged in the long and slow process of rebuilding and restructuring both visible and invisible infrastructures. Central to this process is the involvement of local communities including the youth in the rebuilding process. This can be extremely difficult given the recent past and the experiences of violence on both sides. Youth and community work must therefore be proactive and creative in their approach to future development. As Grattan and Morgan argue:

> the youth [and community] worker is in a unique position to empower young people in the democratic political process. It is particularly critical in situations when communities are either in the process of 'divergence', moving towards conflict, or 'convergence', in the process of reconciliation and reconstruction. Youth [and community] workers of and from the indigenous communities can be a catalyst for understanding. (2007:173)

Given that the young people are both the victims and perpetrators of the violence, it is incumbent upon youth work to initiate forums and relationships that allow young people to express their inner conversations and discuss how to respond to them. If they do not listen to or engage in positive outlets, potentially negative social responses may reignite hatred and violence. Young people must become the future through understanding their past and present and reaching out and to being open to the views of the 'other'. This will be a long and painful process for all involved.

As the cases reported here from NI and BaH show, both societies are still deeply divided by their history and their recent past: both are attempting to rebuild and reconstruct, to engage and develop, in the globalising world. Young people especially are struggling to reconcile the demands of global and local forces that create pressures in a fast changing world. But the examples here show that young people are open to embracing diversity, difference, inclusion and understanding if they themselves are understood, included and valued. Politics has been a major aspect of the conflict in both societies, and both are highly politicised environments. Youth and community development work should recognise that it unevitably has a political dimension. Whether in conflict environments or not, talking and understanding achieve more than killing. Only once the killing stops can the talking begin. The examples described in this chapter illustrate that peace-building and progress can only be achieved if young people are in the forefront of political and decision making processes.

References

Archer, M S (2007) *Making our Way through the World: Human Reflexivity and Social Mobility.* Cambridge: Cambridge University Press

Bowyer Bell, J (1993) *The Irish Troubles: A Generation of Violence, 1967-1992.* Dublin: Gill and MacMillan

Berezin, M (2002) 'Secure States: Towards a political sociology of emotion'. pp33-52 in Barbalet, J (ed.) (2002) *Emotions and Sociology.* London: Basil Blackwell

Conteh-Morgan, E (2001) Globalisation and Human Security: A Neo-Gramscian Perspective. *The International Journal of Peace Studies.* Vol. 17 (2) pp1-16

Coogan, T P (1995) *The Troubles: Ireland's Ordeal 1966-1995, and the Search for Peace.* London: Hutchinson

Di Giovanni, J (2005) *Madness Visible: A Memoir of War.* London: Bloomsbury

Gallagher, T (2004) After the War Comes the Peace? An Examination of the Impact of the Northern Ireland Conflict on Young People, *Journal of Social Issues* 60 (3), pp629-642

Grattan, A (2007a) The Search for Identity in the Face of Diversity: The Case of the Protestant 'Loyalist' Community of Northern Ireland. *The International Journal of Diversity in Organisations, Communities and Nations* Volume 6 (4) pp50-59

Grattan, A (2007b) Reflexive Modernisation, Existential Anxiety and Sense of Identity: An Exploration of 'Perceived' Identity in Crisis. *The International Journal of Diversity in Organisations, Communities and Nations* Volume 7 (4) pp61-71

Grattan, A and Morgan, S (2007) 'Youth Work in Conflict Societies: From Divergence to Convergence.' pp165-175 in Magnuson, D and Baizerman, M (eds), (2007) *Work with Youth in Divided and Contested Societies.* Rotterdam: Sense Publishers

Hamilton, J, Radford, K and Jarman, N (2004) 'Learning to Listen' – Young People and the Police in Northern Ireland, *Youth and Policy* 84, p5-1

Hanson, U (2005) *Troubled Youth? Young People, Violence and Disorder in Northern Ireland.* Belfast: Institute for Conflict Research

Hargie, O, Dickson, D and O'Donnell, M (1998) *Breaking Down Barriers: Sectarianism, Unemployment and the Exclusion of Young People in Northern Ireland Society.* Belfast: University of Ulster

Magnuson, D and Baizerman, M (eds) (2007) *Work with Youth in Divided and Contested Societies.* Rotterdam: Sense Publishers

Malcolm, N (1996) *Bosnia: A Short History.* London: MacMillan

McGhee, D (2005) *Intolerant Britain? Hate, Citizenship and Difference.* Maidenhead: Open University Press

McKittrick, D and McVea, D (2001) *Making Sense of the Troubles.* London, Penguin Books

McMullan, M, McShane, L and Grattan, A (2006) *It's Always in the Back of Your Mind.* Belfast: YANI

Muldoon, O T (2004) Children of the Troubles: The Impact of Political Violence in Northern Ireland. *Journal of Social Issues* 60 (3), pp453-468

Poulton, H (1994) *The Balkans.* London: Minority Rights Publications

Reilly, J Muldoon, OT and Byrne, C (2004) Young Men as Victims and Perpetrators of Violence in Northern Ireland: A Qualitative Analysis. *Journal of Social Issues* 60 (3) pp469-484

Sennett, R (1974) *The Fall of Public Man.* Cambridge: Cambridge University Press

Youth Action Northern Ireland (2004) *Making it r world 2.* Belfast: YANI

Youth Action Northern Ireland (2001) *Everyday Life: Young Men and Violence.* Belfast: YANI

PART 2

8

Housing and community cohesion in rural areas

Tim Brown

Introduction

This chapter highlights the neglected issue of housing and community cohesion in rural areas. A series of reports, academic studies, and media coverage has raised the profile, but they have lacked depth. The specific coverage of housing was inadequate and guidance for policy makers and practitioners at best limited.

The chapter is based on a literature review of recent national policy orientated reports, journal articles and books, supplemented by additional primary and secondary material from a range of sources. These include housing market assessments; thematic regional studies and interviews and discussion with key stakeholders plus a seminar held at De Montfort University in July 2007.

The geographical focus is England and specifically the Midlands. There are important different dimensions to this debate in Scotland and Wales. For example, in rural Wales there are long-standing issues on the impact on traditional communities and culture of second home ownership. There are also concerns in other western European countries on community cohesion in rural areas. In the Netherlands, for instance, there are specific challenges over 'irregular immigrants' in several rural border areas and their impact on housing in small towns and villages.

The chapter goes on to review the coverage of housing and community cohesion in rural areas. The objective is to identify and analyse the overlapping factors that have contributed to a small but growing interest in community cohesion and housing in rural areas, reflected in national and regional policy reports, academic research, media coverage and publicity on good practice examples. This review is followed by an analysis of emerging issues including the need to clarify what is meant by 'community cohesion', the chapter concludes with an agenda for moving forward policy making and research.

The policy perspective

From a national point of view, there are a range of policy drivers that have generated increasing interest in housing and community cohesion in rural areas. These have included the work of the Commission on Integration and Cohesion with the final report noting that there is a 'newness of diversity' post 2001 census in rural areas (Commission on Integration and Cohesion, 2007b: 31). It emphasises that diversity can have a negative impact on cohesion but this is dependent on local circumstances. It therefore suggests that one type of area where further work is required is 'rural areas that are starting to experience diversity' (p9).

This inquiry overlapped with work undertaken by the Institute for Public Policy Research (IPPR) for the Commission for Racial Equality (now the Equalities and Human Rights Commission) on 'the reception and integration of new migrant communities' (Pillai *et al*, 2007). It focused on 'the changing map of diversity in Britain' and commented that 'areas that had previously not known much immigration have received relatively large numbers of newcomers' (p6). According to the authors, this presented major challenges for local authorities and stakeholders that traditionally have not engaged with the community cohesion agenda. A key finding was the difference between perception and reality among sections of the host community. There was a belief that the influx of new migrants had a negative effect on local housing markets specifically affordability in the private sector and accessibility in the social rented sector, though respondents acknowledged that these frustrations reflected a wider concern about a growing rural housing crisis. Apprehension was also expressed about the impact of new migrants on the private rented sector particularly the growth of unlicensed houses in multiple occupation (HMOs).

The Audit Commission (2007) published a report emphasising the benefits of migrant workers for local economies but that this process varied in different parts of the country. It highlighted that this was making community cohesion and ethnicity a significant issue for some areas for the first time, especially rural local authorities. From a housing viewpoint, it emphasised that a proactive approach was needed with a focus on tackling issues in the private rented sector.

The statutory code of guidance on housing was updated by the Commission for Racial Equality (2006). Although it emphasised the changing legislative framework and continuing evidence of discrimination, it noted that geographical patterns of ethnicity were more diverse because of new migrants and refugees. Also that integration and community cohesion were becoming high profile issues for housing organisations that had not traditionally focused on this topic. From a policy perspective, it stressed that local authorities and housing associations might be unlawfully discriminating against ethnic minorities by restricting housing in rural areas to local people (Inside Housing, 2006).

There have also been a number of more specific studies on the impact of international migration especially from A8/A2 countries. The East Midlands Development Agency (EMDA) commissioned work on this topic (Green *et al*, 2007). Although this study was not explicitly focused on rural areas or community cohesion, it showed that between 2002/03 and 2005/06, the number of overseas nationals registering for National Insurance (NI) purposes rose by nearly 200 per cent in the east Midlands compared with 90 per cent for the UK. There was evidence that the trend was towards greater spatial dispersal of migrants, leading to high rates of growth in rural areas, especially Boston and South Holland, with the former having the second highest percentage of overseas people with NI registrations in the region compared with employed residents (19%).

Finally, the Commission for Rural Communities (2007) found that there was a pronounced seasonal trend with a peak registration of migrant workers in rural England in late summer. In terms of geographical distribution, there was evidence that rural areas in the Midlands were experiencing especially high levels of A8 migrants. There were high ratios of registrations relative to the size of the local labour force in rural Lincolnshire, Warwickshire, Wychavon, Herefordshire and parts of Shropshire. From a housing and community cohesion perspective, the Commission for Rural Communities commented that there were concerns about overcrowding in the private rented sector and in tied accommodation, which is housing provided by employers, employment agencies or gangmasters. It also highlighted the use of caravans and temporary accommodation for those in seasonal agricultural work, which was often regarded by local communities as poorly managed and creating an environmental nuisance. The Commission for Rural Communities (2007:7) concluded that 'there is evidence of some tensions and hostility against and amongst migrant workers in some areas'.

Academic research

The research on community cohesion and rural housing from an academic perspective is slowly increasing. It arises from two sources – the disciplinary area of rural studies and the housing needs of black and ethnic minority communities.

The rural studies approach has centred on identity and culture in the countryside and is illustrated in the work of Neal and Agyeman (2006). This investigates the issues of ethnicity, identity and racialised exclusion in rural areas. It adopts a qualitative approach and explores the growing diversity of rural areas, focusing on geography and specific groups like Gypsies and Travellers. It contrasts the perceived picture book idyll of the countryside and the socially constructed image of rurality with the lived space ie the contrasting experiences of different groups living in rural areas, especially 'new' groups. From a policy perspective it raised challenges over social exclusion, racial discrimination and the lack of consideration for equality in policies operating in rural areas.

More generally, the concept of an idealised and romanticised view of rural life continues to have powerful repercussions for policy. Rural society is viewed as based on harmony and stability where the inhabitants enjoy deep and fulfilling relationships. Threats posed to traditional ways of life such as large-scale residential development and in-migration are seen as having a negative impact. At the same time the inadequacy of funding for small-scale affordable housing provision in villages is highlighted as it also represents a challenge to the vitality and vibrancy of rural society, especially where it reinforces disinvestments in public and private sector services such as primary school closures, loss of post offices and cut-backs in public transport.

Nevertheless the qualitative approach which is sometimes referred to as a 'cultural turn in rural studies' is not an uncontested area. Milbourne (2007) argues that alongside such approaches, a return is needed to a quantitative approach so that there is a fuller understanding of population and household movements in rural areas. Although not explicitly focusing on community cohesion, his comment on the lack of adequate data and the limited analysis concurs with the views of Green, Jones and Owen (2007) and the Commission for Rural Communities (2007) about A8/A2 migrants.

From a black and ethnic minority housing perspective, a key development is the examination of 'minority ethnic housing experiences in small town England' (Reeve and Robinson, 2007). As the authors point out, there have been a vast number of studies in large urban areas and they estimate that out of 218 place geographically-based studies, none were in small or medium cities or in rural areas. Yet, the frequently quoted statistic that 5.4 per cent of the black and minority ethnic population live in settlements of less than 10,000 people and that 21 out of the 25 districts that experienced the largest relative increase in size of population between 1991 and 2001 were rural, including a number in the Midlands.

Media coverage

Overlapping with policy studies and academic research, the national media has drawn attention to the issues of community cohesion and housing in rural areas through coverage of a number of events in contrasting ways. These include, gangmasters and the housing and working conditions in the seafood industry (Pai, 2006). This can be contrasted with the case of Tony Martin, a Norfolk farmer, who fortified his semi-derelict property against potential burglars. He shot two intruders, killing one of them. Both, according to the media, came from a Gypsy and Traveller background. Although the majority of coverage focused on the issue of using reasonable force to protect property, there was also an emphasis on the loss of the rural idyll because of in-migration to rural areas. For an overview of the case, see BBC News (2003).

An issue that has spanned policy, academia and media has been the now abandoned attempt by the Government to house asylum seekers in purpose-built accommodation centres in rural areas. The more balanced coverage highlighted the fears of both the local host population and refugees themselves (Hubbard, 2005, Information Centre about Asylum and Refugees, 2003 and Sales, 2007). It was nevertheless treated with considerable hostility by the popular press (Travis, 2002).

More generally, media coverage of the report of the Commission on Integration and Cohesion (2007b) highlighted the rural dimension. *The Guardian* headline on 14 June 2007, 'Racial strife more likely in country villages than big towns, says report', is indicative of the coverage. Similarly, the *Local Government Chronicle* (2007) noted that 'rural towns face risk of community tension flare-ups'. More in-depth media analysis focused on the growth of seasonal migrant agricultural workers in Herefordshire and Worcestershire as well as community tensions between Portuguese households and host communities in Boston during the European Soccer Championship in 2004. The accuracy of some of the reporting is questionable, but only one relatively small part of the Commission's findings received such attention.

There is also some literature which suggests that the issues are not just a recent occurrence, eg Hubbard (2005). An example of this appears in *Housing Today* (2003:26), where a feature article pointed out that:

> In the past four years, some 1,000 Portuguese workers have settled in the market town of Boston. They have jobs, but many need housing – and they could all do without 'taking our jobs and homes' rhetoric of a vocal minority.

Good practice

There are numerous good practice guides and examples and also toolkits in the broad area of housing and community cohesion. Reference has already been made to examples in national reports such as the Commission on Integration and Cohesion (2007b). Other agencies promoting similar material include the Chartered Institute of Housing, the Commission for Rural Communities, the Improvement and Development Agency (IDA), the former Housing Corporation through its innovation and good practice unit (IGP), the Housing Quality Network (HQN) and the Institute of Community Cohesion (ICoCo).

An initial review of these materials plus interviews with a few stakeholders suggest a disappointing picture of the rural scenario. Blackaby (2004:11) stressed the importance of housing as part of the community cohesion debate

> The role that housing can make to community cohesion covers a number of housing activities: development, sales and lettings, housing management and support services.

However, this good practice guide had few if any examples drawn from rural areas. The update by Perry and Blackaby (2007) falls into a similar trap. Similarly, the Housing Corporation IGP Unit had supported nearly 100 projects on community cohesion, but there were less than ten that explicitly or implicitly focused on rural areas. The Housing Quality Network produces a regular series of briefing papers – one of which, centres on housing and community cohesion but there is no reference to the rural dimension (Hayward, 2007). The toolkit section of the ICoCo website does not include a rural category while the housing examples are all exclusively large city orientated. IDA has a specific section of its website on community cohesion: few if any examples are associated with rural areas.

The exception to this negative picture is the Commission for Rural Communities website on migrant workers. Nevertheless in discussions with local stakeholders there was a lack of awareness of this resource. There was a greater knowledge of urban-based examples in national policy reports such as the Commission on Integration and Cohesion (2007b) and the Communities and Local Government (2007) publication on 'what works'.

Community cohesion: an overview

The objective of this section is to explore the relevance of community cohesion for housing in rural areas. The starting point is clarifying its meaning and distinguishing between broad and narrow approaches. This is followed by a brief review of existing definitions.

A useful starting point is a comment by the Commission on Integration and Cohesion (2007a:10):

> We recognise that many tensions are linked to visible differences or difference in cultural practice and that existing residents can feel uncomfortable with 'newness' or change. But we have seen that differences and tensions can arise between people from different age or income groups, different political groups and within the boundaries of single ethnic groups. This makes integration and cohesion 'everybody's business'. It is about the tensions that define a locality and the work that has to be done to mediate those tensions. This is why integration and cohesion is as important in largely white middle class areas as it is in the inner city.

This quotation implicitly identifies and distinguishes between a narrow definition based around ethnicity and a broader focus centred on a variety of differences. The relevance of the narrow definition of integration and cohesion for geographical areas that have traditionally not focused attention on ethnicity is helpful. On the other hand, the wider approach helps to focus attention on the range of differences and tensions in rural areas, such as conflict over housing provision including affordable accommodation. This is illustrated by coverage of 'nimbyism' (not in my backyard) and 'bananas' (build absolutely nothing anywhere near anyone) between wealthy newcomers and traditional residents. As Neal and Agyeman (2006) noted, there are advantages in contrasting the rural idyll image associated with pastoralism and the romantic movement of the eighteenth and nineteenth centuries, with that of a working countryside linked to the modernisation of agriculture and related industries.

On the other hand, as Newby (1980) comments, there is a danger of over-simplification because of the large number of overlapping stakeholders in rural areas. A complex pattern of interests and tensions exists between different types of landowners (eg traditional landed estates, agri-business sector, city investors etc) and different social groups (eg agricultural workers, middle class newcomers, second home owners, the squirearchy etc). The underlining meanings of the countryside are often more complex than simply the rural idyll: for wealthy newcomers as it is often associated with home as a sanctuary as illustrated in the media coverage of the Martin case above and as an investment as well as with the notion of rural community and neighbourliness that is being bought into.

Defining community cohesion is thus a contested area. The most frequently cited policy-orientated definition has been that of the Local Government Association (2002). It identified five principles: a common vision and sense of belonging, an appreciation of the diversity of people's backgrounds and circumstances, a prospect for similar life opportunities irrespective of background, and the development of strong and positive relationships in the workplace, schools and neighbourhoods. The Commission on Integration and Cohesion (2007b:10), however, defines community cohesion as consisting of six elements:

- A clearly defined and widely shared sense of the contribution of different individuals and different communities to a future vision for a neighbourhood, city, region or country
- A strong sense of an individual's rights and responsibilities when living in a particular place
- Similar life opportunities and access to services and treatments irrespective of background
- A strong sense of trust in local institutions to act fairly and to be subject to public scrutiny
- A strong recognition of the contribution of both those who have newly arrived and those who already have deep attachments to a particular place
- Strong and positive relationships between people from different backgrounds in the workplace, in schools and other institutions within neighbourhoods

A major issue is the need to operationalise this definition especially in rural areas. This raises specific concerns in the context of existing rural policy. They include the relatively poor access to services in sparsely populated areas, and the pattern of dispersed workplaces, schools and other institutions in rural areas, an agenda for achieving rural community cohesion will thus be different from an agenda for large cities.

Existing understanding: a stock take!

Previous sections have identified a number of issues on housing and community cohesion in rural areas. These are discussed below in relation to data and information, policy and practice and conceptual frameworks. The national context is also significant in that the issue of community cohesion is a priority as highlighted in the coverage of the final report of the Commission on Integration and Cohesion (2007). Much of the debate from a policy and practice perspective has centred on A8/A2 migrants. There is a danger that other issues become neglected, such as sites for Gypsies and Travellers and the housing needs of old rather than new migrants (Reeve and Robinson, 2007).

There is a general consensus that quantitative data is inadequate. This is illustrated by the caveats provided by Green, Jones and Owen (2007) and the Commission for Rural Communities (2007). Similarly Richardson (2007)) has commented on the inadequacy of data on the different groups of Gypsies and Travellers. The majority of Gypsy and Traveller accommodation assessments (GTAAs) in the east and west Midlands have reached similar conclusions. In relation to ethnicity, Reeve and Robinson (2007) reiterate many of the comments made on urban-orientated black and ethnic minority housing studies about the over-reliance on the census and its limitations in relation to classifying households. From a housing perspective, the guidance on housing market assessments from Communities and Local Government recommends that the needs of black and ethnic minority communities should be included. However, many of these studies do not appear as yet to have focussed on this issue in the rural east and west Midlands. The strategic sub-regional housing market assessments in Lincolnshire and Shropshire have focused on mainstream housing and planning issues at the expense of an analysis of the changing population and household composition in relation to community cohesion and ethnicity.

Previous sections have highlighted the small but growing interest in housing and community cohesion in rural areas. There are two dimensions: good practice examples and policy and practice issues. There is a paucity of accessible good practice case studies. From a substantive policy and practice viewpoint the literature reviewed in the previous sections identifies a number of common areas of concern that are relevant to housing organisations and the community cohesion agenda in the Midlands. At present, there is little robust information and analysis to support or challenge the perceptions of local communities (for example, Pillai *et al*, 2007). These are:

- Impact of rapid and recent changes in the number of migrant workers on the local housing market. Sub-regional and local housing market analysis in rural areas should clearly be addressing this issue. One specific unknown factor is the extent to which A8/A2 migrants will return to their country of origin as a result of the economic recession.

- Implications for the private rented sector. There is some evidence of a significant increase in the number of unlicensed HMOs as well as more anecdotal stories of landlords buying up private property to let out to migrant workers. This might be having indirect effects on the ability of other households to access the private rented sector as well as raising the threshold price for entering the owner occupied market.

- A refocusing of the concept of tied accommodation for meeting the needs of migrant workers. There are a number of dimensions including temporary tied accommodation linked to seasonal employment in agriculture and related occupations, and housing owned by gangmasters. There is a paucity of research and policy on this topic.

- The implications for local authority housing services of a change in the composition of the customer base and the types of issues that need to be addressed, such as homelessness.

- An emerging issue of the difficulty of gaining entry to social housing in rural areas though A8/A2 migrant workers are unlikely to be able to access housing association and council property.

- Growing pressure on the activities of voluntary sector housing organisations such as citizens advice bureaux that traditionally have provided advice services.

Two additional factors emerge from the review of the literature. First, there is considerable variation between localities. From discussions in the west Midlands, there is data that highlights a significant rise in the number of A8 migrants in both north Shropshire and Wychavon. But the nature of the issue is different in that much of the recent growth in numbers in Wychavon is for seasonal employment which requires temporary accommodation, while in north Shropshire it is focused on employment in food processing and general building trades and the need for more permanent accommodation. Second, and more importantly, the key question is analysing the extent to which the perceived issues are adding to the existing housing crisis in rural areas. In some situations there may be various other factors that are worsening the performance of the housing market, such as changing patterns of commuting to urban areas, growth of second homes and the phenomenon of buy to let and buy to invest. Determining the relative importance of these factors are major challenges, especially as national rural housing studies have neglected the migrant worker dimension. The Affordable Rural Housing Commission (2006) and the Matthew Taylor Report (Taylor, 2008) emphasised the growing crisis in the countryside but made little attempt to investigate ethnicity and community cohesion.

A brief review of the academic literature has identified the potential of using contrasting images of the countryside for setting the scene and understanding the tensions around community cohesion. The conflict between the rural idyll and a modern working countryside provides a useful starting point. However, there is a danger that this approach may oversimplify the processes in operation and lead to a bi-polar viewpoint. The reality is of complex and overlapping belief systems.

Moving forward

We have a clear and consistent picture of the gradual acknowledgement of a rural dimension on housing and community cohesion but the lack of any in-depth analysis. The final section of this paper, puts forward an agenda for taking forward policy making and research. It is not intended as a comprehensive proposal. Instead, five interrelated issues and challenges are identified.

- Changing socio-demographic and diversity profiles: There is a lack of quantitative evidence on recent changes as well as limited coverage of long-term population and household movements. Housing market assessments have marginalised this topic. Analytical techniques have been developed but there is a paucity of good quality data. There are few suggestions on how this gap can readily be filled unless local authorities carry out data capture exercises

  Unless a co-ordinated approach is taken on research, it is inevitable that it will consist primarily of qualitative case studies rather than adopting a balanced methodology incorporating statistical analysis of population and household change

■ Literature review: Although there is a growing interest in community cohesion in rural areas, much of the mainstream evidence base is superficial and anecdotal. There is, however, an indication that a range of unpublished reports exists, held principally by local authorities, housing associations and third sector agencies. It would be of value to researchers, policy makers and practitioners to investigate these sources in more depth.

■ Housing issues: as the previous section has indicated there is some evidence to suggest that there are a number of specific issues. These include the role of the private rented sector and the activities of landlords. A detailed specific study on the private rented sector in rural areas would be of considerable value to policy makers and practitioners.

■ Local housing markets: this chapter has shown that national reports and media coverage are increasingly concerned about the impact of rapid changes in patterns of diversity on local housing markets. These also ought to be addressed through housing market assessments but there is little evidence of this.

Forceful guidance from national organisations is needed to remind councils and their partners that housing market assessments should focus on community cohesion and ethnicity.

■ Conceptual frameworks: there is potential to locate research on housing and community cohesion within well-established frameworks in rural studies such as the tension between the rural idyll and the modern countryside. This has the potential to generate useful insights to better inform our understanding of community cohesion and provide a clearer framework for policy intervention.

The relationship between housing and community cohesion in rural areas has begun to be appreciated. But there is a danger that it will continue to be ignored by many academics, policy makers and practitioners. Unless there is a concerted attempt to address the issues set out above, there is little prospect that the inadequate housing conditions and poor quality of life faced by excluded groups such as Gypsies and Travellers and migrant workers in rural areas will be tackled.

References

Affordable Rural Housing Commission (2006) *Final Report.* London: ARHC

Audit Commission (2007) *Crossing the Borders – Responding to the Local Challenges of Migrant Workers.* London: Audit Commission

BBC News (2003) Timeline – The Tony Martin Case http://news.bbc.co.uk/1/hi/england/norfolk/3087003.stm (accessed 14th June 2009)

Blackaby, B (2004) *Community Cohesion and Housing.* Coventry: CIH

Commission for Racial Equality (2006) *Statutory Code of Practice on Racial Equality in Housing – England.* London: CRE

Commission on Integration and Cohesion (2007a) *Our Interim Statement.* London: Commission on Integration and Cohesion

Commission on Integration and Cohesion (2007b) *Our Shared Future.* London: Commission on Integration and Cohesion

Commission for Rural Communities (2007) *A8 Migrant Workers in Rural Areas.* Cheltenham: CRC

Communities and Local Government (2007) *What Works in Community Cohesion.* London: CLG

Green, A, Jones, P and Owen, D (2007) *Migrant Workers in the East Midlands Labour Market,* Coventry: University of Warwick, Warwick Institute for Employment Research

The Guardian (2007) Racial strife more likely in country villages than big towns, says report http://www.guardian.co.uk/society/2007/jun/14/societybriefing (accessed 14 June 2009)

Hayhurst, W (2007) *Housing and Community Cohesion.* York: Housing Quality Network

Housing Today (2003) Far from Home – Rural Immigration, 16 May pp26-29

Hubbard, P (2005) 'Inappropriate and Incongruous' – Opposition to Asylum Centre in the English Countryside. *Journal of Rural Studies* Vol 21 pp3-17

Information Centre about Asylum and Refugees (2003) *Understanding the Stranger.* London: ICAR

Inside Housing (2006) Restrictive Rural Policies May Push out BME Groups, 8th September

Local Government Association and Institute of Community Cohesion (2007) *Estimating the Scale and Impacts of Migration at the Local Level.* London: LGA

Local Government Association (2002) *Guidance on Community Cohesion.* London: LGA

Local Government Chronicle (2007) Rural Towns Face Risk of Community Tension Flare Ups, 7 June

Milbourne, P (2007) Repopulating Rural Studies – Migration, Movements and Mobilities. *Journal of Rural Studies* Vol 23 pp381-386

Neal, S and Agyeman, L (eds)(2006) *The New Countryside – Ethnicity, Nation and Exclusion in Contemporary Rural Britain.* Bristol: Policy Press

Newby, R (1980) *Green and Pleasant Land? – Social Change in Rural England.* Harmondsworth: Penguin

Pai, H-H (2006) Another Morecambe Bay is Waiting to Happen http://www.guardian.co.uk/commentisfree/2006/mar/28/comment.immigration (accessed 14 June 2009)

Perry, J and Blackaby, B (2007) *Community Cohesion and Housing – A Good Practice Guide.* Coventry: CIH

Pillai, R, Kyambi, S, Nowacka, K and Sriskandarajah (2007) *The Reception and Integration of New Migrant Communities.* London: IPPR

Reeve, K and Robinson, D (2007) Beyond the Multi-Ethnic Metropolis – Minority Ethnic Housing Experiences in Small Town England. *Housing Studies* Vol 22 No 4, pp547-572

Richardson, J (2007) *Contentious Spaces – The Gypsy/ Traveller Site Issue.* Coventry: CIH and JRF

Sales, R (2007) *Understanding Immigration and Refugee Policy.* Bristol: Policy Press

Taylor M (2008) *Living Working Countryside: The Taylor Review of Rural Economy and Affordable Housing.* London: CLG

Travis A (2002) Minister Stirs Row Over Plans for 15 New Centres http://www.guardian.co.uk/uk/2002/may/15/immigration.immigrationandpublicservices2 (accessed 14 June 2009)

9

Policing experiences and perceptions of new communities in Britain

Perry Stanislas

Introduction

This chapter is part of a proposed study examining the perceptions and experiences of new Polish and Somalian migrants of British policing. It examines how British society impacts on these communities, whether this colours their policing experiences and if so in what way. And whether their experiences and perceptions of policing in countries other than Britain influence their views of the police service in Britain. The chapter does not examine the Polish or Somalian police but takes account of certain key issues which the empirical work seeks to explore.

I am a tutor and leader of the Diversity and Community Engagement module on the Police Foundation Degree for police student officers. De Montfort University has developed this course in conjunction with Leicestershire Police. Having read countless student assignments on the relationship between the police and new communities, I am frequently struck by the almost unanimous view of police students, albeit generally unsupported by evidence, that new communities' perceptions of the British police are shaped by their experiences of policing before coming to Britain. They assume that those experiences are poor. Similar views have been expressed by police elsewhere (HCCLGC, 2008; Thorp, 2008). For example police services from other countries may be very effective in handling particular issues but less so in others (Mawby, 1996). This is clearly illustrated by the unfair treatment of the Portuguese police by the British media during the Madeline McCann case:

ignoring the abduction of children is literally unheard of in that country, thus problematising foreign police.

Given the wide area of activity covered by policing in most countries (Bowling and Foster, 2002; Mawby, 2005), such generalisations are dangerous. Moreover, these views were expressed by people with little experience of policing, which suggests that the collective group-think associated with aspects of informal police culture may well be influencing these beliefs, or they may be shaped by shared knowledge obtained from any number of sources (Foster, 2005). However, many of the assumptions underlying these views are worthy of critical consideration namely:

- ■ The assumption that the policing experiences of newcomers in their country of origin are inferior to those experienced in Britain and influence present attitudes is not new (Banton, 1964, Holdaway, 1991).

- ■ The notion that newcomers are unable to critically assess British police against previous experience in favourable ways is questionable and promotes a deterministic view of human behaviour (Flick, 2006; Sporton and Valentine, 2007).

- ■ The emphasis on previous police experiences by student officers imposes a uniformity on social groups which may not apply given the differences in age, social status, regional and other demographic characteristics of new communities.

- ■ The assumption that the past is more important than the present serves to marginalise any negative experiences new communities have with the police while in Britain .

Polish immigration to Britain

Many Polish servicemen settled in Britain after WWII. It is estimated that there were 163,000 British-based Poles in 1953 (Castle and Kossack, 1973; Drinkwater *et al*, 2006). The 2001 Census found less than 61,000 Polish born people living in Britain, with 57 per cent being over 64. Despite being relatively low-key, Polish communities are well established in areas such as Bedfordshire and Leicestershire. St Paul's Church in Leicester, founded by ex-servicemen in 1948, serves as a hub for members of the Polish community and there are similar institutions in areas such as Melton Mowbray[1].

The existence of a settled British Polish community with its infrastructure and support networks was seen as important in attracting new Polish communities after the 2004 Accession Act came into force (Sales, 2002; Drinkwater *et al*, 2006:5; Murdie, 2008). The Act expanded membership of the European Union

(EU) to eight countries (the A8 nations), including Poland, granting the legal right to work and live in member states. The poor Polish economy drove immigration (Mawby, 1996) and Poles, more than other EU nationals, took advantage of the provision to enter Britain and establish their own business or be self-employed. From 1999 significant numbers of Poles entering the country as tourists were able to seek residency in Britain, unlike those from Hungary and other A7 countries, who had to apply from their home countries (Drinkwater *et al*, 2006). As well as those legally entitled there are also estimated to be a high number of illegal migrants, making it difficult to determine the size of the Polish community – an issue which interests government agencies (Drinkwater *et al*, 2006:6; Robinson *et al*, 2007).

The Work Registration Scheme (WRS) established by the government to handle members of the A8 nations wishing to work, excluding the self-employed, provides information which is helpful in understanding trends within this group. Poles are the largest A8 immigrant group in Britain, as illustrated by their higher numbers on the WRS with 264,560 followed by Slovakians with 44,300 in 2006 (Home Office *et al*, 2006). These figures represent those successfully accepted on the WRS, not the applications.

Polish immigrants share characteristics with many economic migrants. The majority of registered A8 workers are single people with no dependents, aged between 18-34 years old (Dustman and Fabbri, 2005; Home Office *et al*, 2006). The top five occupations for registered workers are in administration and business management (34%), hospitality and catering (21%), agriculture (12%), manufacturing (7%) and food, fish and meat processing (5%). Some 66,000 Polish workers are to be found in east Anglia, 58,000 in London and 51,000 in the Midlands.

There are 12,000 employed in administration and business in London with approximately 30,000 in hospitality and catering. In the Midlands approximately 27,000 Poles work in administration and business etc, with 6,000 or so working in hospitality and catering. Ninety seven per cent of registered workers work full-time, even though they earn less than indigenous people given their levels of education and training, especially when compared against white Commonwealth immigrants (Drinkwater *et al*, 2006) but this may be a temporary state of affairs. In some occupational areas, like construction and self-employed tradesmen, Poles are in direct competition in cities with members of other ethnic minorities such as African-Caribbeans (Modood *et al*, 1997; Dustman and Fabbri, 2005:458).

Social problems and issues

Like most economic migrants operating in a new environment, Polish workers generally seek accommodation through fellow immigrants who have been in the country longer, not necessarily from British Poles of long standing (Robinson *et al*, 2007). The issue of safety and receptiveness is important, as Robinson *et al*, (2007:10) spell out: 'These immigrants were found to have rapidly developed nuanced mental maps of the city that included notions of safe places and hostile spaces'.

Many migrants prefer areas where there is ethnic diversity: this is against a background of widespread anxiety about and hostility to A8 migrants from sections of indigenous communities. According to the Federation of Poles in Great Britain, this has contributed to a sense of persecution (Wilby, 2008). The difference between recent immigrants and those from the Commonwealth in earlier periods is that migration to Britain was spread over a longer period of time (Berkley *et al*, 2006). As a consequence the media, especially newspapers like the *Daily Mail* with its long history of racism and anti-immigrant senti-ment, have created a political focus on new migrants that is more intense than at any point in recent history (Patel, 2002). The media has focused on new groups entering the country, be they legal economic workers, asylum seekers or illegal migrants; including individuals trafficked by criminal gangs (Sales, 2002; Slack and Drury, 2008).

Policing

The problemisation of the A8 community was explicit in the comments of Chief Constable Julie Spence of Cambridgeshire Police. Her words were used by the media (Slack, 2008) in what appears to be the orchestration of a moral panic (Jewkes, 2004). Spence argued that her police force could not cope be-cause of insufficient resources for policing these new communities. Little was said about the positive contribution being made by immigrant workers to the country (Berkley *et al*, 2006). Spence has been joined by many politicians, in-cluding high-profile black public figures such as Chief Constable Mike Fuller of Kent Police and the chair of the Equality and Human Rights Commission Trevor Phillips (Stanislas, 2009; Wright, 2008). Spence identified a list of offences or issues of concern which she associated with immigrant com-munities (Solivetti, 2005). She asserted a proclivity amongst Poles and Lithuanians *inter alia* for carrying knives, within the context of media generated frenzy about knife crime. She purported that Eastern European criminal elements tended to use violence in debt recovery, exploiting fellow migrants, and claimed that a significant rise in drink and driving offences was due to different attitudes to this in certain EU countries (Thorp, 2008:98).

While the Association of Chief Police Officers (ACPO) were quick to dismiss the remarks of their colleague as evidentially unfounded (Dodd, 2008; Slack, 2008), this response may have been as political in character as Chief Constable Spence's (Sales, 2002; Berkley *et al*, 2006; *The Telegraph* 16 April 2008). While Spence said little about the crimes being committed against migrant communities, painting them largely as offenders by default (Goodey, 2003: 417), the impression given by ACPO's rebuttal of her claims could incorrectly imply that the changing nature of British society does not constitute a challenge to the police and other agencies (HCCLGC, 2008).

ACPO have robustly maintained that European immigrants' involvement in crime is no higher than that of the indigenous population: the question of whether this is correct or only comparative has been raised from many quarters (Martens, 1999; *The Telegraph* 16 April, 2008). Using the comparator of the older Commonwealth immigrant community suggests a potentially different set of conclusions, although they are tentative and exploratory, in terms of levels of victimisation or participation in crime (Bowling and Phillips, 2003; Stanislas, 2006; Stanislas, 2009). It took a couple of decades after Caribbean migration to Britain before mugging became popularly associated with African-Caribbean youth, and much longer before Africans or Asians became linked with particular offences (Tonry, 1999; Goodey, 2003: 417, Stanislas, 2009b). In terms of experiences of crime, racial victimisation was commonly experienced by Commonwealth immigrants and there were a number of fatalities (Bowling and Phillips, 2003). However, an internet search of newspapers suggests that the number of Poles who have been victims or involved in serious crime appears potentially higher than for older immigrant communities. This pattern has formed within a shorter time and applies particularly to crimes against women, even if they are statistically small and in line with figures in the general population.

For example, Polish student Aneta Kluk was sexually assaulted and killed in Glasgow (Laville and McLaughlin, 2006) and 26 year-old Sylwia Sobczak was murdered, decapitated, and her body burned (*Sky News* 19 May 2008). In Liverpool two men were accused of killing and setting alight a young Polish woman (*Liverpool Daily Post* 15 January 2008). Similar murders of Polish women have taken place in Bedfordshire and other parts of the country (BBC News 16 April 2007). It may well be that migration creates certain risks for women from within their own ethnic group as well as outside it (Dunhill, 1989).

One example of an offender is female care-worker, Jolanta Kalinowsica, who brutally murdered her elderly Jewish employer and stole her money (*The Mail on line* 7 March 2008). While there is no evidence that the victim's ethnicity played any part in her fate, the issue of the racist attitudes of many Eastern European immigrants towards other new communities as well as established British ethnic minorities has been observed (Thorp, 2008:98; McDowell, 2009). In addition, elements within new communities may have a greater involvement or exposure to unlawful activities than previous generations of immigrants, especially in the context of illegal immigration and organised crime (Sales, 2002; Goodey, 2003,).

Calls for a European-wide police database by those supporting Spencer's sentiments (Slack, 2008) and the need for a European-wide DNA database recommended by her detractors, including the ex-Commissioner of the Metropolitan Police (Computing, 2008) suggest shared concern about A8 offenders, even if they diverge on the percentages of crime they are believed to contribute to (Thorp, 2008).

The British police need to carry out their work with EU migrants more effectively, assisting with serious problems of homelessness and with language barriers (Robinson *et al*, 2007:86). Their ability to ascertain the offending backgrounds of those on British soil has caused some concern (ACPO Progress Report Undated). It is evident that Polish immigrants are more offended against in terms of hate crime, gender-based violence, or other offences, most of which go unreported (Bennetto, 2009:6), than offending (Slack and Wilby, 2008). This is further highlighted in the bizarre deaths of two Polish farm workers in Hereford (Bowen, 2008) or the death of a drunken Pole who was held in police custody for domestic violence (BBC News, February 9 2008).

Somali immigrants in Britain
The Somali community is among the oldest groups of immigrants to settle in Britain. Liverpool and other port cities formed the hub of early Somali communities in Britain, along with West African and Caribbean seamen (Elam and Chinouya, 2001; Stanislas, 2009). The overwhelming majority of contemporary Somalis in Britain are refugees from the troubles in their home country, with the more educated or prosperous fleeing to other western countries such as the US, Canada *inter alia* (Murdie, 2002). Those from north Somalia who were more exposed to British systems and language were more likely to seek refuge in these countries, while the more Italianised southerners sought safety in Italy or Switzerland (Fisher, 2004; Booth, 2005).

The majority of Somalis live in London: a quarter of the young were born in Tower Hamlets, one of the few older communities of ex-seamen with relations with the newcomers, and most have refugee status (Elam and Chinouya, 2001; Robinson *et al*, 2007). Refugee communities have also grown up in Manchester and the Midlands. While the 2001 Census found 44,000 Somali born residents in the UK more recent research places the figure closer to 95,000 (Harris, 2004).

Social issues and problems

Unlike legal migrants, refugees have no right to work or access to the welfare state until they are granted Exceptional Leave to Remain. The inability to work and earn money immediately diminishes the power of individuals to determine where they live and is often the start of a long process of temporary relocations in inappropriate accommodation, homelessness, and desperation (Sales, 2002; Robinson *et al*, 2007:86). Racial harassment is a common experience of Somali refugees especially when they are accommodated in predominantly white communities, such as northern cities. Some Somalis, however, report their safety and acceptance in many parts of the country (Sporton and Valentine, 2007).

Those fortunate to find permanent accommodation are often housed in unpopular and poor housing estates (Murdie, 2002; Robinson and Rees, 2007: 86) such as in Tower Hamlets, which is one of the poorest boroughs in the country and home to a major Bengali population (Harris, 2004). Despite less severe harassment in multi-ethnic areas, Somalis still experience difficulties from both white and other communities, such as African-Caribbean youth who view them as 'homeless' and as culturally distinct (ie not black) in terms of dress, faith and language. That many older Somalis identify with Arabs and disassociate with Africans can create tension with the established majority African-Caribbean and West African groups (Elam and Chinouya, 2001:45) and this is underscored by the latter's antipathy towards Islam. This contrasts with the social affiliations within older seaport communities where greater commonalities were found (Stanislas, 2009).

The length of the time they are unable to work is resented by Somalian refugees, as it feeds the racist impression of their being dependent on the state, which is culturally alien to Somali society (Harris, 2004). According to the 2001 Census, 70.4 per cent of Somalis are economically inactive (ICAR, 2007). This popular media image of dependency misrepresents the strong values of autonomy amongst Somalis, evidenced in the fifty or so businesses catering for their community in one London high street alone, rivalling more established minorities (Sales, 2002; Harris, 2004). In addition, Somali men are constrained by discrimination in the workplace and, like West Africans, are unable to find employment commensurate with their education and training. They are up against the hierarchy of colour, class and culture which governs British society (Modood, 1990; Elam and Chinouya, 2001; Stanislas, 2006).

Disadvantages experienced by white immigrants appears to be temporary, whereas those faced by non-white immigrants are more enduring (Dustmann and Fabbri, 2005). For many of them immigration to Britain usually involves the decline in social status and a reduction of personal freedom (Stanislas, 2006), whereas white EU immigrants can move about without harassment (Robinson and Rees 2006:82). Somali men are particularly badly affected by discrimination because it attacks their cultural norms concerning masculinity.

All this contributes to domestic tensions, violence, mental health issues and drug use (Elam and Chinouya, 2001; Sales, 2003:467; Sporton and Valentine, 2007:17). This dynamic is not unique to Somalis and is seen in its most extreme form in the African-Caribbean family (Stanislas, 2009). The rise in a single parent families and other changes in the family structure has increased the number of young people at risk or involved in crime. Westernisation and the values of British society undermine the internal regulatory capacity and authority of many non-white families and communities, weakening cultural capital (Stanislas, 2006; Stanislas, 2009). This can be seen in children's ability to threaten the intervention of white agencies such as social services, in disputes with their parents. Similarly, wives are able to undermine their husband's authority by opportunistically threatening police intervention within an environment which privileges the accounts of women and where ethnic minority communities are viewed as quintessentially sexist and more prone to domestic violence. These almost colonial attitudes are evident in the assignments of many police students (Stanislas, 2009).

Policing

Despite the exposure to racial victimisation experienced by Somalis, they soon become associated with crime by the national media. This is part of a broad process of criminalising new communities by giving special attention to offences involving them (Goodey, 2003:417). When the stabbing of 15 year old Somalian Asema Dawit by an obsessed Eritrean stalker gained much media coverage the report was set in the context of intense coverage on knife crime underscored by the racial origins of the offender (*The Daily Mail*, 4 June 2008). More commonly Somalis are portrayed as suspects or offenders. Bowling and Phillips (2003) and Benneto *et al* (2009) highlight the significant increase in the use of police stop and search powers and anti-terrorist legislation against non-white males to rationalise traditional practice prior to the terrorist attacks on 7 July 2005 and thereafter. Somalis and other new immigrant groups are more likely to attract police attention because of uncertainty about their legal status.

The involvement of a Somali gang in the shooting and killing of police officer Sharon Beshenivsky in 2005 in the process of carrying out a robbery (*Times Online* 9 November 2005) reinforced this association between this new community with violent crime. The thwarted terrorist bombings involving a group of Somalis led to arrests in London and Italy (Booth, 2005). Somalis are unique amongst African nationals in all sharing one religion: they are Shiite Muslims. Moreover, Somalia has been accused of harbouring and training anti-western terrorists (Vasagar, 2007). The disaffection of many young Somali males, like their elders, is reflected in their poor school performance or disinterest in education (Elam and Chinuoya, 2003). Their involvement in 'gangs' has its origins in being targeted as a new minority group by other ethnic minority groups at school, and this spills out into the wider community (Asthana and Townsend, 2006).

Many of these gangs are similar to other ethnic youth affiliations in large British cities, involved in drugs and robbery and often leading to violent intra and inter ethnic disputes (Stanislas, 2009). This was highlighted in a documentary by journalist Raghi Omar on Channel 4 in 2008 entitled *Immigration the Inconvenient Truth*. One example of gang feuds involved the son of ex-Ugandan dictator Idi Amin: Faisal Wangita, along with approximately 40 mostly older Somali men violently attacked and killed 18 year-old Somali Mahir Osman. While Wangita received a five-year sentence, the three Somali ringleaders were sentenced to life because of their extreme and callous violence (Laville and Mclaughlin, 2007). The level of violence involved in this and other crimes by Somalis has led the police to conclude that much of it is influenced by trauma or exposure to extreme violence in a war-torn country, (Elam and Chinuoya, 2003). The predictability of these events is that the focus on violent masculinity dominates discussion of the policing needs of the Somali community in many large cities, at the expense of other issues of concern to the wider community or in other parts of the country.

Conclusion

The new Polish and Somalian refugees in Britain both experience significant hostility to their presence from sections of the host society, even though such attitudes have historically been reserved for non-white communities. In this case, the different status of migrants does not spare them from hate crime.

While such racism comes from traditional sources, Somalis have attracted enmity from black youth also, who view their presence as an encroachment on established and contested patterns of relations.

Potentially disturbing and requiring more research is the notion that hostility to newcomers may take a gendered form. Polish women appear vulnerable to sexually-based predatory attacks from those outside their ethnic group. This raises the spectre of these women being at risk from traditional domestic abuse and from predatory violence on the streets. Their skin colour is no protection.

The restrictive conditions placed on the Somali community by government policy seem questionable and threaten to reproduce crimogenic conditions similar to those associated with the African-Caribbean community. These are characterised by problems of masculinity and adaptation, familial instability and the growing involvement of young males in crime. Little has been learnt from experiences of older migrant communities: short-term political expediency outweighs the multiple costs to society. This highlights how government policy makes many non-white families dysfunctional.

In terms of policing it is important to establish how the needs of new migrant communities reflect those of the host society or differ from other ethnic minority communities. Ethnically based violence occurs in both the Polish and Somalian communities, as it does in established British ethnic minority communities. They also have in common communication and language barriers and the way this limits their access to services and legal rights, and impedes the police's ability to engage appropriately with them in an educational context or as victims or offenders. For offenders, the existence of organised crime gangs, stemming from old Eastern bloc countries which prey on A7 migrants, makes it ever more pressing for the police and researchers in the field of policing to develop appropriate responses.

References

Asthana, A and Townsend, M (2006) Knives Rule the Playground as Inter-Racial Violence Soars. *The Observer*, 4 June

Banton, M (1964) *The Police in the Community.* London: Tavistock

bbc.co.uk (2007) Man Denies Murdering Polish Woman, 16 April

Bennetto, J (2009) *Police and Racism: What Has Been Achieved 10 Years After Stephen Lawrence Inquiry Report?* Equality and Human Rights Commission. London

Berkley, R Khan, O and Ambikaipaker, M (2006) *What's New About New Immigration in the Twenty-First Century Britain?* Joseph Rowntree Foundation

Booth, J (2005) All Four Bombers in Custody After Dramatic Raids, www.timesonline. 31 October, Accessed February 2008

Bowen, M (2008) Marden Farm Double Death Update, *Hereford Times*, 29 June

Bowling, B and Foster, J (2002) Policing and the Police in M Maguire, R Morgan and R Reiner (ed) *The Oxford Handbook of Criminology.* Oxford University Press

Bowling, B and Phillips, C (2003) *Race and Crime in Britain.* London: Longman

Castle, S and Kosack, G (1973) *Immigrant Workers and Class Structure in Western Europe.* Oxford University Press

Computing (2008) *Met Police Chief Calls for European DNA Database*, 5 March

Dodd, V (2008) Migrant Crime Wave a Myth-Police Study Reveals, *The Guardian*, 16 April

Drinkwater, S, Eade, J and Garapich, M (2006) Poles Apart? EU Enlargement and the Labour Market Outcomes of Immigrants in the UK. *IZA Discussion Paper Series* No 2110

Dustmann, C and Fabbri, F (2005) Immigrants in the British Labour Market, *Fiscal Studies* Vol 26, Issue 4

Elam, G and Chinouya, M (2001) *Final Report on Feasibility Study of Health Surveys Amongst Black African Populations Living in the UK.* London: Department of Health

Fisher, I (2004) Somalis Find a New Kind of Hardship in Italy, *The New York Times*, 31 October

Flick, U (2006) *An Introduction to Qualitative Research.* London: Sage

Foster, J (2005) Police Cultures, in T Newburn, *The Handbook of Policing.* London: Willan Publishing

Goodey, J (2003) Migration, Crime and Victimhood: Responses to Sex Trafficking in the EU in *Punishment and Society,* Vol 5, Issue 4

Harris, H (2004) *The Somali Community in the UK: What We Know and How We know it* (ICAR) London

Holdaway, S (1991) *Recruiting a Multi-Racial Police Force.* London: Home Office

Home Office, Department for Works and Pensions and HMS Revenue Customs and Department for Local Government, (2006) *Accession Monitoring Report*

House of Commons Communities and Local Government Committee. *Community Cohesion and Migration* (2008)

ICAR (2007) *Briefing: The Somali Refugee Community in the UK, Information Centre for Asylum Seekers and Refugees*

Jewkes, Y (2004) *Media and Crime.* London: Sage

Laville, S (2007) Big Daddy's Boy: Idi Amin Son Jailed Over Somali Gang Murder, *The Guardian* 7 August

Laville, S and McLaughlin, D (2006) Sister Criticises Police After Murdered Student's Body is Found in Church. Guardian.co.uk, 2 October Accessed February 2008

Mail Online ((2008) Polish Shopper Who Murdered Elderly Employer Then Went on Shopping Spree Jailed for 20 Years, 7 March Accessed February 2008

Martens, P (1999) Immigrants, Crime and Criminal Justice in Sweden in M Tonry (ed) *Ethnicity, Crime, and Immigration: comparatives and cross national perspectives.* University of Chicago Press

Mawby, R (1996) *Comparative Research of Police Practice in England, Germany, Poland and Hungary.* Solvenia: College of Police and Security Studies

McDowell, L (2009) Old and New European Migrants: whiteness and managed migration policies. *Journal of Ethnic and Migration Studies*, Vol 35, No 1

Modood, T, Berthould, R and Lakey, J (1997) *Ethnic Minorities in Britain: Diversity and Disadvantage.* London: Policy Studies Institute

Modood, T (1990) Catching UP with Jesse Jackson Being Oppressed and Being Somebody. *New Community,* Vol 17, No 1

Murdie, R (2002) The Housing Careers of Polish and Somali Newcomers in Toronto's Rental Market. *Housing Studies,* Vol 17, Issue 3

Patel, P (2002) Back to the Future: avoiding de ja vu, in Anthias, F and Lloyd, C (ed) *Resisting Racism.* London: Routledge

Robinson, D, Reeve, K and Casey, R (2007) *The Housing Pathway of New Immigrants.* Joseph Rowntree Foundation

Sales, R (2002) The Deserving and the Undeserving? Refugees, Asylum Seekers and Welfare in Britain, *Critical Social Policy* Vol 22: p456

Slack, J and Drury, I (2008) All Party Call for Cap on Migrants. *The Daily Mail,* 8 September

Solivetti, M L (2005) Counterblast: Who is Afraid of Migration and Crime? *The Howard Journal,* Vol 44 No 3

Sporton, D and Valentine, G (2007) Identities on the Move: The Integration Experiences of Somali Refugee and Asylum Seeker Young People. *The Economic and Social Research Council*

Stanislas, P (2006) Models of Organisation and Leadership Behaviour Amongst Ethnic Minorities and Policing, Unpublished PhD Thesis. University of London

Stanislas, P (2008) Black Masculinity, Culture, and Violence. Unpublished Paper

Stanislas, P (2009) The Cultural Politics of African-Caribbean and West African Families in Britain, in C Hylton and B Oshien (ed) *The Black Family as a Site of Struggle.* Manchester University Press

Stanislas, P (2009) Pre and Post Colonial Discourses and Policing Violent Homophobia in the Caribbean and the British Caribbean Diaspora. Unpublished paper

Thorp, A (2008) *Impacts of Immigration.* House of Commons Library, Research Paper 08/65

Times Online (2005) Teenager Charged With Murdering WPC, 29 November

Vasagar, J (2007) Somali Islamist Held UK Meeting to Raise Funds. *The Guardian,* 13 January

Wilby, P (2008) A tale of prejudice. *The Guardian* 11 August 2008

Wright, S (2008) Top Black Cop Warns of 'Migrant Crime Surge'. *The Daily Mail* 28 January

Note

1. www.leicestershirevillages.com accessed 7 August 2008

10

Crabs in a barrel: race, class and widening participation

Carlton Howson

Education is the passport to the future, for tomorrow belongs to those who prepare for it today. Malcolm X (1925-1965)

This chapter is based on observations and research and reflects the gap that still exists between social groups. These gaps affect entry to higher education institutions (HEIs) and retention of Black and white working-class students and creates a disparity in degree attainment and progress into the world of employment. This chapter explores some of the stories behind an emerging theme suggesting that white working-class people are now the most endangered group in relation to education. It argues that the HEI is often portrayed as the bastion of equality, a place that promotes and enhances the capacity of its members and graduates, where they can be exposed to difference in a collegiate manner, and where they can learn to challenge discrimination and discriminatory practices. The Executive Summary of a DFES report *The Future of Higher Education* (2003) speaks about the value of higher education

> Our higher education system is a great asset, both for individuals and the nation ... Universities and colleges play a vital role in expanding opportunity and promoting social justice. The benefits of higher education for individuals are far-reaching. On average, graduates get better jobs and earn more than those without higher education. (DFES, 2003)

John Denham then universities secretary said that Higher Education can 'help unlock the talent of their local people' and that:

> Never have universities and colleges been more important to our country both nationally in ensuring our success on the world stage and locally in our towns and cities through the creation of jobs and new skills, driving regeneration and enriching cultural life. (BBC News, 2008)

Some two hundred years after the end of transatlantic slavery, the relationship between Black and non-Black people is still marked by conflict and tension based on the nature of relationships and on competition where Black people are competing under rules that were designed to keep them hostage to those who control the game (Lammy, 2007). This game, played out in many public spaces and the classroom, remains a classic example of the struggle between academics and academics, academics and students, and students and students. Thomas observed that:

> Classrooms are no longer a congregation of learners receiving information from a teacher, but a microcosm of discrete and overlapping manipulative struggles for status, respect, and ... ethnic hostility, degradation rituals, ... contests, and power-dominating games. (Thomas, 1993:44)

Where tutors leave students to their own devices, the extent of this struggle is often glossed over (Rubin, 2003; Fox, 2004). Instead of leadership and challenge there is an apparent myopia when it comes to recognising and setting out effective strategies for minimising the kind of discriminatory behaviour experienced in classrooms (Thomas, 1993). Staff will often resort to some notion of neutrality or objectivity and fail to recognise or articulate how they are involved in the manipulation of an educational process. This system ultimately manifests itself as class wars, where classrooms are an extension of wider society, aping a society which constantly shifts the debate, reinventing itself as a custodian of rights and justice, whilst presiding over all forms of inequality and injustice that cause participants to take direct action to resolve their everyday struggle (Young, 1990; Žižek, 2002).

This chapter argues that despite numerous policies aimed at challenging discriminatory practices within the public services to reduce social and economic inequalities, little has changed (Lindle, 2008). The situation remains bleak as the relationship between Black and non Black people remains distrustful with everyone apparently sceptical of measures taken to increase racial harmony and equality (Engberg, 2004; Aspinall and Mitton, 2007). This seems an anomaly when a Black man holds presidential office in a powerful nation. The result of the presidential elections in the USA has given weight to the idea of meritocracy. Barack Obama is seen as someone who has achieved greatness by his own efforts. This event challenges some commonly held views about the social construction of race and the ideology that has been used to sustain it (Smaje, 1997; Ladner, 1998; Archer, 2001; Watts and Erevelles, 2004; Guess, 2006).

The campaign in the two years leading up to the election revealed some commonly held notions in relation to social class, Black people, women and privilege (Mazama, 2007; Walters, 2007). That Obama is now US President continues to unite and fragment people. 'Yes we can' is now the anthem used to rally the disenfranchised, invoking within them the audacity of hope: others are waging a 'war of position' as they seek to reclaim the economical and political discourse and decision making for the neo-liberals and elite groups (Kalb, 2005).

One recognises the juxtaposed position of Obama and the intersectionality of 'race', class, gender, sexuality, faith, disability and age: all these characteristics as identifiers of membership of particular social groups were brought into question during the presidential elections. Obama is the manifestation of several groups: a man of mixed parentage, with a Muslim sounding name and a Muslim father, who ran against a white woman in his own party. Thus the issues of race, gender and faith were important during the election campaign. Obama's personal and political identity was being constructed and deconstructed and this meant that he had to assert himself as the best person for the job based not on ethnicity, gender, class, sexuality, disability or faith but rather on his ability and his audacity to run for President. Since his election we note that he has had to avoid being drawn on issues pertaining to 'race' and racism, leaving it to others to articulate that which seems patently obvious.

This President is being scrutinised, his every move examined to see whether he has the ability to deliver on his election promise; can he mend a society that has become so fractured, a society that is so ready to implode, so ready to self-destruct? The struggles of Obama are now global struggles that manifest themselves in the minutiae or the management of concerns such as security and the economy. The economic insecurity and increased terrorist threats are politically induced (Huddy, Fieldman and Weber, 2007; Evans, 2008; Melander, 2009; Ostrowidzki, 2009), reflecting how oppositional politicians are setting an agenda to maintain their political and physical hegemony (Aradau and Munster, 2007; Evans, 2008; Ostrowidzki, 2009).

Yet ordinary people are more concerned with a different struggle. They find themselves competing for health care, housing, jobs, social services and education. They too are interested in sustainable economic and global security;

they struggle to hold on to what many political leaders appear to have lost sight of. However the mismanagement and abuse by politicians, in relation to the use of public funds for their own advantage, the credit crunch, pensions and the war on terror have led to high levels of distrust, and individualism nurtured by the politics of neo-liberalism which has been a feature of the last three decades (Sivanandan, 2006a). The nurturing of individualism was championed as an exercise of greater freedom, where people were able to choose and in making their own choices would be liberating themselves from dependence on the state. In reality this was a smokescreen which caused some to lose sight of other commitments such as restoration of justice, equality and love. Some might even argue that far from creating community cohesion, the measures have increased both class and racial tension and disharmony among some groups (Bosworth and Guild, 2008).

What is significant here is that one is drawn to the racial tension, with little attention given to the social and economic consequences for groups who are trapped in locations in which they feel neglected, forgotten, unimportant or where they are terrorised by the lack of necessities. In such circumstances the strategy utilised by the state is to find a plausible scapegoat and there is no better scapegoat than one who shares the same space. They are a visible manifestation of what you have been taught to hate; they are real, you notice them when you are in a queue, when you attempt to get health care, social security, housing, jobs and education. They are uninvited space invaders, they come into your space to take what you have, what you desire, what you need. They then disappear but they always return in ever increasing numbers and within a climate of diminishing resources until it seems reasonable to react and find ways to dissuade such groups from further advances. In this scenario both Black people and white are manipulated, invisiblised or highlighted, as befits the intentions of the manipulator.

The recent Local and European elections witnessed significant advances by far right political parties (BNP), mainstream political parties were forced to review their misalignment. As a result one fully expects further manipulation by the state. The strategy of disorientation is important because once people become disorientated, they become more susceptible to control, and the narrative about the economic crisis and the inability of the major public services to deliver are presented as having to do with 'others'. Thus a 'them' and 'us' doctrine is developed, and the process of 'othering' becomes manifest in government policy (Sivanandan, 2006a). The articulation of this form of othering, manifest in government and academic discourse, becomes the focus for those people excluded from the knowledge, who rely on servants of the state, the educators who distil the script they are given to make it more plausible, making it seem logical to favour your own, in a climate of fear, poverty or oppositional politics. One begins to make sense of the antics of crabs in a barrel (Goodhart, 2004).

The advancement of the British National Party will be used to suggest that the country has become more racist. And rather than challenging this notion, mainstream political parties are likely to become even more robust in their desire to show that they are in control; intensifying the war on people, rather than the war on poverty, utilising the rhetoric of a war on terror to justify further measures for control. Increased surveillance of staff and students in higher education (HE) and increased controls of immigration are some examples of these measures (Reynolds, 2002; BBC news, 2002; Hogan, 2004; Ashely, 2007; Newman, 2008). The discourse from the state will adopt tried and tested methods of divide and conquer, capitalising on the rhetoric of the BNP as it panders to a small but vocal minority who lament about St. George's flag and being British and the extent to which those people who feel that they have ownership of a country, a way of life based on tradition, have themselves been disenfranchised. This is a powerful message to politicians because it means that the articulation of policies on welfare and the control of the movement of people will form a significant part of manifestos for the next election. We will witness further examples of crab in a barrel antics as politicians attempt to persuade the electorate that they are sensitive to the issues that are of concern. One can expect to hear proclamations about searching to reconcile difference, equity and justice. Crabs in a barrel emulate the reactions of people when resources are severely limited.

Widening participation

Higher education has witnessed expansion over the last three decades to a point where its value is questioned, its ambition to widening education further is challenged. And in the present climate it may be forced to contract, leaving many groups not traditionally part of the educational elite vulnerable.

The workings of capitalism, inequality and resultant poverty impact adversely on the quality of the lives of both Black and white working-class people. Yet despite the negative aspects of capitalism, it is still seductive because people brought up within capitalist systems tend to be greedy: greed creates the drive, the desire. Moreover, lack of choice means that people are forced to make transactions with the recognised currency. We are aware that Black people and working-class people occupy a space often vacated by others. Black and white working-class people who can change their market position are often used by the state to affirm their educational and community co-hesion policies. Thus, when people are positioned in relation to their social and economic capital, working-class people both Black and white are in trouble.

The deviation between white working-class people and Black people is due to racism. Racism impacts on Black people in ways that many white people can-not imagine and many remain complicit in what is generally seen as the actions of the few. Whilst racism is endemic in society, the explicit articulation and behaviour of those considered to be racist is attributed to the beliefs, attitudes and behaviour of a few and not to the wider indigenous white popu-lation who are regarded as more tolerant. The negative behaviour is dismissed as due to ignorance, and education is seen as the cure. The well-educated who crave positions of influence often utilise their position for their own interest and many of those whose background is working-class find themselves de-fending their new prestigious positions and acting against the interest of other working-class groups.

In an effort to change the conditions of their lives, working-class people both Black and white invest in education, driven by what Mirza (2006; 2009) calls educational desire; they subject themselves to another form of distortion and possible alienation from themselves as they seek to gain the opportunities that seemed to be reserved for the upper middle-class and elite groups. This is significant because education historically has been used as a finishing school – a place that teaches graduates how to live within the expectation of their position. Many follow the footsteps of their parents and their position within the capitalist structure of dominance is assured. Graduation from HE symbolically affirmed their position: educational attainment as justification for social inclusion and social position.

The expansion of higher education is seen as an attempt to reduce the gap between social groups, especially where the gap is determined more by ethni-city, gender and wealth than any other factor. This expansion of education may act as a foil, an illusion of equity between different social groups. The im-portance of education in relation to social position and enhanced oppor-tunity is shown by the competition for places at what are perceived as the best performing institutions. In any hierarchy there will be those who exist at the top and those who are perpetually at the bottom. The idea of one group out-performing another has been the *status quo* from the inception of state edu-cation. The normative position has favoured white middle-class men. How-ever white women have closed the attainment gap and this, along with the enhanced attainment levels of some ethnic minority groups, has raised concerns about the location of white working-class males.

What is of specific concern is how the relative attainment level between Black and white working-class people is being evened out. The attainment level of women and Black people challenges previous social constructions about intelligence and ability based on gender and ethnicity, such as the salience of men or patriarchy and white supremacy. Implicit in the discourse about widening participation, education and social policy is the notion that Black people are receiving preferential treatment over white working-class people. Yet it could be argued that the widening participation agenda was primarily aimed at white working-class people.

In a report entitled *Who Cares about the White Working Class?* Sveinsson (2009) notes that Britain has remained dominated by class division and that people are scornful of the perceived notion of the culture of white working-class people. However the report also disputes the claim that white working-class communities have been directly losing out to visible Black and or ethnically minoritised people (Travis, 2009). A recent report undertaken by the Institute for Public Policy Research (IPPR) on behalf of the Equality and Human Rights Commission has also argued that the idea of immigrants queue jumping or being given priority in social housing is largely based on perception rather than reality (*Guardian*, 2009).

The continual distillation of these ideas may result in a reaction against Black people, fracturing an already fragile and delicate balance between the groups. The fragility of the relationship between the Black and white working-class was tested in the disturbances in the north of England in 2001. This led to the now infamous Community Cohesion Policy (Home Office, 2001), which some believe was intended to be a means of controlling the movement of Black and ethnically minoritised people. It also illustrated the Government's perception and lack of response to the problem of poverty and inequality (Ashrif, 2007; Thomas, 2009). Closer scrutiny of the events that contributed to the main post-war uprisings shows that poverty was a factor in that Black and non-Black people found themselves struggling for the same meagre public services. All were excluded from policy making, all are manipulated within a capitalist system and all are utilised by suggesting that one group's condition is a result of the others'. This manipulation keeps these groups occupied; like crabs in a barrel they struggle for a way out and this diverts attention away from the source of their adversity.

Organisations such as the British National Party have capitalised on this by representing themselves as the party who cares for white British people. The BNP and its allies has conveniently forgotten how 'English imperialism, has seeped into everyone's culture' and how, as Monbiot (2009) suggests,

> British imperialism ... has destroyed the sense of a discrete and self-contained nation. The values, language, governance and business structures, the global integration we imposed on other nations have come back to bite us. (Monbiot, 2009)

The BNP and its allies fail to see the links between its imperialistic past and the presence of Black people; they have argued that immigration and the presence of large numbers of Black people or other migrants work against the interest of the white working-classes. This argument resonates with increasing assertions of this nature and diverts attention away from the source of the problem.

In a response to these concerns former Communities' Secretary, Hazel Blear reportedly said:

> Britain remains blighted by class division, and economic background is still the best predictor of life chances. Class is central to how people see their place in Britain today. (Blears, in Travis, 2009)

The educational hierarchy has the potential to provoke enormous hostility and enmity between social groups. The post-war enlightenment period has led to vociferous campaigns about enhancing opportunities by exposing inequality and increasing diversity. This has evoked greater scrutiny of persisting patterns in, for example, the take up of services, employment and attainment. These patterns have led some to identify inequality and injustice as the main determinants (James, 2008). Closer examination reveals that ethnicity, gender, class and disability are the main areas in which disparity in attainment is most evident. The absence of data in some areas makes comparisons difficult; there are similarities in the discriminatory practices which impact adversely on particular groups. Recent publications talk about a narrowing of the gap in relation to gender (see Richardson, 2007) but this may require further scrutiny. A discourse is emerging about the plight of the white working-class community; this is a triumph for those who have continued to argue about the prevailing power of social class in Britain even when recent Prime Ministers have attempted to discount the resilience and significance of class inequalities (Toynbee, 2009; Travis, 2009).

What is particularly interesting however is that the present discourse is now racialised. White people are seen as a particular ethnic group, a group that is now the subject of particular forms of discrimination and oppression that were previously the preserve of ethnic minorities. Women, disabled people, lesbian, gay, bisexual and transgender (LGBT) people, and people with mental health issues are some examples of groups against discrimination. These groups were all outside the construction of normal, though 'normal' was never defined, simply assumed. The fact that normal was not defined enabled those in power to assert that people who had particular characteristics or behaviour patterns face predictable outcomes such as that ethnic minority and working-class people are more likely to obtain lower levels of attainment or terminate their course of study.

Those who hold power, wealth and status are in a position to commission research to confirm the predictions made about another group. Many researchers find themselves – willingly or reluctantly – contributing to rationalising inequality and using science as the ultimate justification. This supposedly objective assessment, then, is not about 'race', racism, gender, or a desire to harm any particular social group; it is about recognising and articulating an inconvenient truth about the propensity of some groups actually to harm themselves in the manner in which they live their lives.

One of the most glaring concerns is the extent to which a process of othering is established. The discourse on Whiteness, in particular the extent to which some white people are represented as the new marginalised group which is alienated due to the progress of some ethnic minority groups, is postulated by people from all sides of the political spectrum. The idea of dark strangers as the problem is presented as a diversion from the main course of the deep and intractable social, economic and structural disease that erodes life chances for Black and white working-class people (Smith, 2008; James, 2008). These dark strangers are regarded as living parallel lives to those who live within the borders but who are selective in what aspects of the culture and or services they choose; those who are apparently doing as well as, if not better than white indigenous communities. There is little challenge to these generalisations. The depersonalisation of people becomes significant in that they have been categorised into 'white' (and right) or 'Black' (ethnically minoritised people including migrant workers, asylum seekers, refugees, Gypsies, Travellers and immigrants).

This discourse is articulated with little explicit reference to ethnicity or government policy, yet it is evident from the reaction of people on various points along the political spectrum that there are highly charged emotions associated with the idea of poor white families being further disadvantaged as a result of Black people who do not deserve so much support (Green, 2001). One reaction is the recent election of BNP councillors in what were regarded as 'safe' Labour seats: the BNP has significantly increased the number of its members elected to serve on local councils and the European Parliament. Labour MP Jon Cruddas warned that:

> With Ukip faltering, few local elections and the economy hurtling into recession, we will need everyone who opposes the BNP's message of hate to play a part. A BNP victory will change the political landscape in Britain. (Cruddas, 2009 in Ryan, 2009)

Several western European countries have seen the emergence of far right parties but it remains unclear whether this is an indication of increased racist activity or just a reaction to some of the policies of the respective governments (Alistair *et al*, 2008). However, the fact that such emotions and hostility can be evoked without actually mentioning particular ethnic groups shows the power of a type of inference known as 'dog whistling'. Calma (2008) quotes Professor Peter Manning and others who debated the term and concluded that dog whistling carries coded messages within language that at one level appear neutral but which at other levels send meanings to different audiences. These embedded messages are often of hate and division and this is 'another subtle, yet mischievous use of language that threatens civil society' (Calma, 2008).

The essence of the discourse is grounded in concerns about losing out to another social group; a social group that has occupied a lesser position within the pyramid system which characterises most western democracies. In many of these places an ideology was established as justification of the relative positions of Black people and white. The social construction of racial superiority – white people – has been fundamentally challenged throughout history. But through the process of appropriating different groups, reducing them to commodities and controlling the curriculum, the educators of the white dominant group have achieved a condition of memory relapse for themselves and others. Carruthers (1995) refers to this as 'selective memory'; a process of claiming the aspect of history that one desires and re-storying it so that one group is brutalised whilst the other simultaneously portrays itself as courageous, gallant and heroic. Writers such as Rodney (1972), Brah (1985), Browder (1992), Khamit-kush (1993), Sallah (2007) and others have given specific accounts of historical accounts which have been distorted in favour of glorifying the role Europeans played in destabilising Africa, India and other places in the world. History is always told by the victors.

The story told about transatlantic slavery is a powerful example; the enslavement of millions of people, shackled and shipped to a far distant land where the violence, rape and mutilation experienced on the voyage was only a precursor to what would be the taken for granted behaviour between social groups. The way in which one group of people regarded or behaved in the presence of the other was dictated by the formal and informal conventions of that time. The behaviour between the groups was normalised, Black people were distrusted and made to feel inferior whilst white people projected themselves as superior. Theirs was an act of compassion, an attempt to bring civilisation to the new world. This type of rhetoric is still common and is often used by political leaders.

Poverty, global warming, corruption, disease and war are the biggest challenges facing humanity; but rather than mounting a collective effort to find solutions, our governments have shown themselves to be impotent and arrogant in the way they have treated people. They have opted for a discordant approach leading to identity politics. Over to the major crises, world leaders have shown themselves wanting; yet they continue their rhetoric whilst pursuing their own agendas apparently with no thought for the everyday concerns of the people they govern. In attempts to deflect attention from their incapacity to make the difference that people crave, they have suggested that our problems are a result of the way certain social groups live their lives. One example of this is how they claim that refugees, asylum seekers and other immigrant groups are the reason why working-class people are neglected. The struggle for identity is distinctive and needs to be applied and analysed within the context in which it emerges. This will inevitably involve a consideration and acknowledgement of a person's legitimate right to be a member of the human family. Difference is not the most important issue: it is what we make of difference; one hand many fingers, different but equal.

Creating the circumstances to facilitate the possibility of a better world is a crucial function of the state. As Calma (2008) says '... if you change a government, you change the nation'. The state can be a catalyst for change with respect to welfare, social services, criminal justice, education and all the major institutions. A process of cleansing through truth and reconciliation is needed, which permeates both public and private spheres to dislocate the historical conditions that gave rise to the present enmity between social groups, produced the sense of disenfranchisement and led to instability and insecurity on a global scale.

Historical, economic, social and political processes not only control, mediate and manipulate the macro aspects of society: they are also played out in micro spaces such as the classroom. Making sense of the space one occupies becomes significant. Identifying and utilising the tools available to students to discover how they situate themselves in relation to how they are situated within that space is essential.

A process of higher education lacks potency if it fails to recognise its responsibility in working with students to change the circumstances that have caused past and present inequalities. Higher education needs to assert itself; it cannot remain passive or hostage to the state and commerce. It needs to recognise its responsibilities in shaping those who can recognise the impending dangers that threaten how we live our lives. The perpetuation of divisions between social groups is a corrosive strategy aimed at control; it is a strategy that leads people to think of themselves on the basis of classifications and categories. They are like a computer barcode or a chip that is synthesised with a person's DNA to predetermine particular behaviour. The ability to create and recreate ought to lead to different outcomes, but the coercive power of the state facilitates the maintenance of a hegemonic grip, forcing participants to cling to their identity, both real and imagined, as a symbol of status and worth. Thus relationships are often codified and mediated within a structure of dominance.

A structure of dominance has consequences for the people who are only seen through the lenses that link them to something considered in negative terms – a pariah or someone who desires the unattainable. We might encourage people with whom we live and work to aspire, to hold on to hope, but people will rationalise their situation based on the symbolic and practical 'real life' interactions they encounter. A structure of dominance demands that people submit to it and education is used to assist in the creation of what Freire (1972) calls a process of 'domestication'.

A system of dominance is like a virus that mutates, making it difficult to recognise or to find an antidote. Within this system there is a discourse about universal values, a rhetoric about social or community cohesion. Some attempt is made to include others, but the terms of inclusion are dictated by the prevailing economic, social and political order. The use of such terms presents a dialectical dilemma for some of its users: language is not neutral, it conveys as much as it conceals; the meanings attached to particular words or ideas will usually have resonance with a context. This is why there is broad political and economic consensus about the use of social inclusion. Calma

(2008) noted that 'social inclusion seems to have now become an all-encompassing term' and that it captures many of the 'government's policy platforms about social equity and fairness'. However, the reality is significantly different for many groups who experience life on the fringe.

It is noticeable that among many students in higher education there is little discourse about social inequality, especially the inequality that exists between students in the same academic institutions and on the same courses. Discussions about difference tend to be superficial or along the lines of cultural tourism, not deviating much from the three S's of saris, steelbands and samosas identified by Chauhan (1989) over 20 years ago.

The face of Europe has many complexions. It is increasingly diverse partly due to mobility but also to enforced migration of those seeking refuge or those seeking to enhance their quality of life by moving to areas regarded as more politically stable and prosperous. For some this has proved to be a case of the grass looking greener. Difficulties arise when curiosity about new neighbours becomes hostility, or when people who are deemed 'different' are only recognised when that difference is seen as an impediment that can be used against them when things do not work in relation to equality (Green, 2001).

The problem seemed to be based not on practice or policies but on the individual's inability to take advantage of what is equally distributed and available to all (Green, 2001). However availability requires the individual to take, rather than wait to be given. In our competitive pyramid system, there is little chance of someone just being given something – they have to earn it. A meritocracy enables all participants to compete for the reward: in higher education the prize is qualifications that lead to careers associated with particular status. However, the theoretical application of this notion does not take account of the insidious ways in which some groups are favoured at the expense of others.

The literature is littered with accounts of the devastating impact when members of social groups that have been othered fail to recognise the material and political reality, entering schemes that seduce them into joining the oppressive apparatus that reinforces the hegemony of the main culture and the ideas postulated to ensure compliance and social cohesion. These groups are enslaved by a distorted perspective (Howson, 2007).

Some have suggested that embracing and embedding diversity in public services means that change will eventually follow (Kandola and Fullerton,

1998). However, a diversity strategy that fails to engage critically in an interrogation of policy, practice and ideology will fail to change the prevailing situation which gave rise to it (Wrench, 2005). Given that many diversity strategies are developed by officers who are mandated to manage the image of the organisation or reduce the potential for litigation against it, we should not be surprised when those to whom we surrendered are seduced by capitalism and are now muzzled, unable to challenge the system they are indebted to. They become assimilated and complicit and are used as tools within the capitalist system to invoke the same fear in others. They hope to escape the insecurity that they invoke on others, but feel compelled to do the bidding of their superiors. Some discover that they can establish a lucrative career by producing research papers that acknowledge that there are difficulties. They want us to focus our attention on those at the bottom of the pyramid, arguing that the main difficulties lie with them, their inadequacy, their culture and their misfortune, rather than with the structural social, economic and political system (Green, 2001).

The difficulty lies with those at the bottom of the pyramid – but why do those at the bottom continue to occupy those positions, and *vice versa*? The answer is complex. Analysis of available data suggests that it lies with both their location and the cause of their location; the two issues are interwoven. That is not to say however that one's social position will inevitably lead to social exclusion. Travis has argued that:

> The white working class are discriminated against because of their accent, style, food, clothes, postcodes. (Travis, 2009)

Discrimination affects people who are situated by physical geography, social construction, and ideology. Social construction has the capacity to produce something that on the surface appears fixed; although in reality it is more fluid, because meritocracy demands that members of society are offered the possibility of enhancing their quality of life and providing an escape from even the most abominable situations.

I am agitated by the accusation that attempts made by Black people to change the conditions of their lives are seen to be at the expense of other social groups; progress has been made not because of government policy but in spite of it. The progress made by some Black groups is comparable to that made by some white groups. However, this progress still leaves Black people on the whole lagging woefully behind white middle class people. Neither is the progress made consistent across the group as a whole. Where there has been progress in Black students' survival in a higher education system that is a microcosm of wider social processes, it is because of the principles and qualities inculcated in them by their parents, teachers and community which promotes self-determination and a refusal to accept what others have determined for them. They embrace the audacity of hope.

The assertion that white working-class people's condition, participation and attainment in higher education is linked to government policy that favours Black people at their expense is perverse. This kind of reasoning perpetuates the division between groups that are affected by the same economic and structural impediments and thus maintains the crab in a barrel antics.

Governments act in accordance with their own agenda and their own vision. At times they may seek to colonise language by hijacking key ideas and shaping the discourse in their own favour, or become donors by offering incentives to groups who align themselves with the state in an attempt to get support. These groups are then compelled to conform to measures of control, so weakening the efforts required to make a difference for their own social group or the issues that they are most concerned about. Government has a huge capacity to spend public money on its consultations, only to come back and tell us what is good for us. Much of what it does can be reduced to rhetoric, action and policy (RAP).

The problem that working-class white people and Black people face is reflected in the experiences they encounter both inside and outside higher education (Bird, 1996). Relationships with tutors often reinforce some of the negative aspects of what is described as 'their culture'; a culture that has been pathologised and hinders them, apparently making them dysfunctional in certain contexts (Travis, 2009). The argument is that '*their* culture' is incompatible with the culture inside and outside higher education institutions and consequently policies aimed at inclusion are not an antidote but merely an inducement aimed at the incorporation of a few. Social inclusion is a tag with an associated set of values that describes how civil society provides opportunity, builds wealth, is sustainable, promotes social harmony, and ensures greater equality and justice for its citizens.

The terms social cohesion and social inclusion are sometimes used interchangeably, as though the two mean the same thing or at least are intended to have the same outcomes. Social inclusion is one aspect of the Widening Participation mantra advocated by the government over the last decade (Jary and Jones, 2006). It ought to embrace a set of values that applies equally to all those for whom we have a moral responsibility: those who are struck by poverty, those who live in an unfavourable postcode area, those who seek protection. It should provide an opportunity to participate in processes, systems, structures and institutions that can facilitate changing the conditions they live in. For, as Donnison notes,

> The inequalities in British society are neither inevitable nor accidental. They are now severe enough to damage every citizen. They are most plainly damaging of our children and young people – preparing them for exclusion from the mainstream of what should be their society. (Donnison, 1998:30)

Human rights are about the inherent dignity that should be accorded all humans, and an approach to social affairs that is based on respect, understanding and communication. To this end educators should see themselves as prospectors panning for gold, diamonds and the genius that exists and is waiting to be shaped.

References

Alexander, B K (2003) (Re) visioning the ethnographic site: interpretive ethnography as a method of pedagogical reflexivity and scholarly production. *Qualitative Inquiry* 9 (3) pp416-441

Alistair, C, Bottom, K and Copus, C (2008) More similar than they'd like to admit? ideology policy and populism in the trajectories of the British National Party and respect *British Politics* 3 (4) pp511-534

Aradau, C and Munster, R V (2007) Governing terrorism through risk: taking precautions, (un) knowing the Future. *European Journal of International Relations* 13 (1) pp89-115

Archer, L (2001) Muslim brothers, black lads, traditional Asians: British Muslim young men's constructions of race, religion and masculinity *Feminism and Psychology* 11 (1) pp79-105

Armstrong, D (2009) Educating youth: assimilation and the democratic alternative in Wood and Hine (2009) *Work with Young People,* Sage

Ashely, D (2007) Lecturers vote unanimously to throw out government spying plans UCU News, 30 May 2007 http://www.ucu.org.uk/index.cfm?articleid=2594 (Accessed June 2008)

Ashrif, S (2007) Uprisings, community cohesion and Muslim Youth in Sallah, M and Howson, C (2007) *Working with Black Young People.* London: Russell House

Aspinall, P and Mitton, L (2007) Are English local authorities practices on housing and council tax benefit administration meeting race equality requirements? *Critical Social Policy* 27 (3) pp381-414

Baxter, J (2002) Competing discourses in the classroom: a post-structuralist discourse analysis of girls' and boys' speech in public contexts. *Discourse and Society* 13 (6) pp827-842

BBC News (2002) EU agrees tighter immigration controls 22nd June 2002 http://news.bbc.co.uk/1/hi/world/europe/2059078.stm (Accessed June 2008)

BBC News (2008) Campuses planned for 20 towns http://news.bbc.co.uk/go/pr/fr/-/2/hi/uk_news/education/7274729.stm (Accessed March 2008)

Bird, J (1996) *Black students and higher education: rhetorics and realitie.* Buckingham: Society for Research into Higher Education and Open University Press

Bosworth, M and Guild, M (2008) Governing through migration control: Security and Citizenship in Britain. *British Journal of Criminology* 2008 48(6) pp703-719

Brah, A (1985) Cultural Encounter During the Raj. *Minority Experience in Ethnic Minorities and Community Relations.* Milton Keynes Open University Press

Browder, A T (1992) *Nile Valley Contributions to Civilization: Exploding the Myths Vol.1*. Washington The Institute of Karmic Guidance

Calma, T (2008) Social Inclusion for New and Emerging Communities National Race Discrimination Commissioner, Opening speech to the 'Making a Difference'. Social Inclusion for New and Emerging Communities Conference Adelaide, 26 June 2008

Carruthers, J H (1995) Afrika and the Afrikans in the 21st Century Video of conference in Manchester England organised by Action on Earth Communications

Chapman, K (1994) Variability of degree results in geography in United Kingdom universities 1973-90: preliminary results and policy implications. *Studies in Higher Education*, 19 pp89-102

Chauhan, V (1989) *Beyond Steelbands 'n' Samosas – Black Young People in the Youth Service*. National Youth Bureau: Leicester

DFES (2003) *The Future of Higher Education*. http://www.dfes.gov.uk/hegateway/strategy/hestrategy/exec.shtml (Accessed: June 2007)

Donnison, D (1998) *Policies for a Just Society*. Basingstoke: Palgrave Macmillan

Engberg, M E (2004) Improving intergroup relations in higher education: a critical examination of the influence of educational interventions on racial bias. *Review of Educational Research* 74 (4) pp473-524

Evans, P (2008) Is an alternative globalization possible? *Politics and Society* 36 (2) p271-305

Fox, J E (2004) Missing the mark: nationalist politics and student apathy. *East European Politics and Societies* 18 (3) pp363-393

Freire, P (1972) *Pedagogy of the Oppressed*. Harmondsworth Penguin

Fryer, P (1984) *Staying in Power: The History of Black People in Britain*. London: Pluto Classics

Giroux, H A (2001) Cultural studies as performative politics. *Cultural Studies and Critical Methodologies* 1 (1) pp5-23

Goodhart, D (2004) Discomfort of strangers. *Guardian* Tuesday February 24 2004 http://www.guardian.co.uk/politics/2004/feb/24/race.eu (Accessed June 2009)

Green, D G (2001) Liberal Anti-Racism. *Prospect Magazine* October 2001 http://www.civitas.org.uk/pubs/prospectOct01.php (Accessed June 2008)

Guardian (2009) Claims that immigrants prioritised for social housing 'a myth' guardian.co.uk Tuesday 7 July 2009 (Accessed July 2009)

Guess, T J (2006) The social construction of whiteness: racism by intent racism by consequence. *Critical Sociology* 32 (4) pp649-673

Higher Education Statistics Agency (2007) *Students in higher education institutions*. 2005/06 Cheltenham: HESA

Hogan, D (2004) the racism of fortress Europe http://flag.blackened.net/revolt/wsm/pamphlets/eu/fortress.html (Accessed June 2009)

Home Office (2001) *Community Cohesion, A Report of the Independent Review Team*. Chaired by Ted Cantle Report

hooks, b (1992) *Black Looks, race and representation*. Cambridge Ma: South End Press

Howson, C (2007) Working with black young people: the development of black consciousness in an oppressive climate in Sallah, M and Howson, C (2007) *Working with Black Young People*. London: Russell House

Huddy, L Feldman, S and Weber, C (2007) The Political Consequences of Perceived Threat and Felt Insecurity *The ANNALS of the American Academy of Political and Social Science* 614 (1) pp131-153

James, O (2008) Selfish capitalism is bad for our mental health *The Guardian* http://www.guardian. co.uk/commentisfree/story/0,,2234337,00.html (Accessed January 08)

Jary, D and Jones, R (2006) Overview of widening participation policy and practice in *Perspectives and Practice in Widening Participation in the Social Sciences* edited by David Jary and Robb Jones http://www.c-sap.bham.ac.uk/resources/publications/monographs/widening_participation/Chapter 1.pdf

Kalb, D (2005) From flows to violence: Politics and knowledge in the debates on globalization and empire. *Anthropological Theory* 5 (2) pp176-204

Kandola, R and Fullerton, J (1998) *Diversity in Action: Managing the Mosaic* (2nd edition). Pern Kandola, CIPD (1998)

Khamit-kush, I (1993) *The Missing Pages of 'His-Story': Highlights in Black Achievement.* New York D & J Books, INC

Kreindler, S A (2005) A dual group processes model of individual differences in prejudice. *Personality and Social Psychology Review* 9 (2) pp90-107

Ladner, J (1998) *The Death of White Sociology.* Baltimore: Black Classic Press

Lammy, D (2007) Speech to the Wilberforce Institute for the study of Slavery and Emancipation in Hull 18 May 2007 http://www.culture.gov.uk/reference_library/minister_speeches/2048.aspx/ (August 2009)

Lave, J (1988) *Cognition in practice.* Hillsdale NJ: Erlbaum

Lindle, J C (2008) Real or imagined fear? *Educational Policy* 22 (1) pp28-44

Mayo, M Gaventa, J and Rooke, A (2009) Learning global citizenship? Exploring connections between the local and the global. *Education, Citizenship and Social Justice* 4 (2) pp161-175

Mazama, A (2007) The Barack Obama phenomenon. *Journal of Black Studies* 38 (1) pp7-29

Melander, E (2009) The geography of fear: regional ethnic diversity, the security dilemma and ethnic war. *European Journal of International Relations* 15 (1) pp95-124

Mirza, H S (2006) Race, gender and educational desire. *Race Ethnicity and Education* 9 (2) July 2006 p137-158

Mirza, H S (2009) *'Race', gender and educational desire.* London: Routledge

Monbiot, G (2009) Someone Else's England Published in the *Guardian* http://www.monbiot. com/archives/2009/02/17/someone-elses-england/ (Accessed February 2009)

Newman, M (2008) Research into Islamic terrorism led to police response, *Times Higher Education* http://www.timeshighereducation.co.uk/story.asp?storycode=402125 (Accessed June 2009)

Ostrowidzki, E A (2009) Utopias of the new right in J G Ballard's Fiction. *Space and Culture* 12 (1) pp4-24

Owen, D Green, A Pitcher, J and Maguire, M (2000) *Minority ethnic participation and achievements in education, training and the labour market.* (Research Report No. 225) London: Department for Education and Skills

Powdthavee, N and Vignoles, A (2007) Succeeding in higher education: a widening participation issue. Unpublished manuscript. Institute of Education University of London

Reynolds, P (2008) Fortress Europe raises the drawbridge *BBC news* 18 June 2002 http://news. bbc.co.uk/1/hi/world/europe/2042779.stm (Accessed June 2009)

Richardson, JTE (2007) *Degree attainment ethnicity and gender. A literature review.* Higher Education Authority

Rodney, W (1972) *How Europe Underdeveloped Africa.* Zimbabwe Publishing House

Rubin, BC (2003) Unpacking detracking: when progressive pedagogy meets students' social worlds. *American Educational Research Journal* 40 (2) pp539-573

Ryan R (2009) BNP wins council seat in Kent *The Guardian* http://www.guardian.co.uk/politics/2009/feb/20/bnp-council-victory (Accessed February 2009)

Sallah, H (2007) *Treatise on Founding a Federation of African Republics People's*. Gambia: Centre for Social Science Research

Sivanandan, A (2006a) Race, terror and civil society. *Race and Class* 47(3) pp1-8

Sivanandan, A (2006b) Attacks on multicultural Britain pave the way for enforced assimilation. *Guardian* http://www.guardian.co.uk/comment/story/0,,1870907,00.html (Accessed October 2006)

Smaje, C (1997) Not just a social construct: theorising race and ethnicity. *Sociology* 31 (2) pp307-327

Smith, D (2008) Editorial: beyond greed, fear and anger. *Current Sociology* 56 (3) pp347-350

Sveinsson, K P (2009) *Who Cares about the White Working Class*. London: Runnymede

Thomas, J (1993) *Doing Critical Ethnography*. California: Sage

Toynbee, P (2009) Equal opportunity is fantasy in any society this unequal. *The Guardian* 20 July 2009http://www.guardian.co.uk/commentisfree/2009/jul/20/social-mobility-inequality-milburn (Accessed July 2009)

Travis, A (2009) Class blamed for bias against poor whites. *Guardian* 22 January 2009

Walters, R (2007) Barack Obama and the Politics of Blackness. *Journal of Black Studies* 38 (1) pp7-29

Watts, I E and Erevelles, N (2004) These deadly times: reconceptualizing school violence by using critical race theory and disability Studies. *American Educational Research Journal* 41 (2) pp271-299

West, Kanye (2004) *Jesus Walks. The School Dropout* Audio CD. Roc-a-Fella

Wrench, J (2005) Diversity management can be bad for you. *Race and Class* 46 (3)

Yorke, M (2002) Degree classifications in English, Welsh and Northern Irish universities: trends 1994-95 to 1998-99. *Higher Education Quarterly* 56 pp92-108

Young, I M (1990) *Justice and the Politics of Difference*. Princeton University Press

Youssef, M (2008) Suffering men of empire: human security and the war on Iraq. *Cultural Dynamics* 20 (2) pp149-166

Žižek, S (2002) *Welcome to the desert of the real*. London: Verso

11

A Multiculturalist Approach for Gypsies and Travellers? How the lack of site provision engenders conflict and promotes assimilation

Joanna Richardson

Introduction

In a society which has focused on a multiculturalist approach to community cohesion, there seems to be a process of forcing Gypsies and Travellers either to conform and assimilate to a settled or house-dwelling norm or to risk being moved on and evicted from unauthorised encampments.

Under the Race Relations Act (1976), Romany Gypsies, Irish Travellers and, towards the end of 2008, Scottish Gypsies are recognised ethnic groups as determined by the courts, for the purposes of bringing cases of race discrimination. However, under English planning law the essence of whether a person is a Gypsy or Traveller has largely depended upon how nomadic they are. This has meant that Gypsies and Travellers need to be nomadic in order to prove their race, yet they are prevented from doing this by a range of legislation and regulation.

In England and Wales, the former Office of the Deputy Prime Minister (ODPM) published its (2005) strategy *Sustainable Communities – Homes for All*; the 'all' does not include Gypsies and Travellers. Since legislation in 1994, they have been prevented from stopping on the road-side and local authorities have been excused from having to provide sites for them. More recent legislation (Housing Act, 2004) has meant that councils must assess the needs of this minority group and outline how provision for them will be included in their local plans. For housing associations and local authorities in England and Wales money is being made available to provide more sites and therefore to include Gypsies and Travellers in this laudable aim of *Homes for All*. However, the discriminatory treatment of the travelling community goes on.

After providing a brief context for the current situation, the chapter embarks on an examination of 'race' and the impact of racism on the treatment of Gypsies and Travellers. Examples of racial discrimination are evident on many levels: in some legislation and its implementation (for instance the Criminal Justice and Public Order Act, 1994) and in societal and media discourse and action (Richardson, 2006).

The chapter discusses the role that housing has to play in providing accommodation for Gypsies and Travellers, particularly in the light of the heightened tension and conflict that debate about sites engenders. This conflict results from Gypsies and Travellers being depicted as 'other', as not 'residing' in communities' – and not as people who should be afforded the protection and respect for cultural differences that are given to other ethnic groups. Resolving this conflict depends upon government, the media and the wider community rethinking the residence issues for Gypsies and Travellers and moving forward with site provision.

The Context for Gypsies and Travellers in England

Gypsies and Travellers live in most member states of Europe and it is estimated that there are approximately ten million people in these groups, across the continent (Gil-Robles, 2006a:4). The size of Britain's Gypsy and Traveller population is also an estimate, with Council of Europe figures putting it at about 300,000, with approximately 200,000 in settled housing (Crawley, 2004:6). There is a variety of work which examines the English history of Gypsies and Travellers; see Acton (1974, 1994 and 2000), Acton and Mundy (1997), Clark and Greenfields (2006), Hancock (2002), Hawes and Perez (1996), Kenrick and Clark (1999) and Mayall (1995).

Defining Gypsies and Travellers as a group in legal terms has been difficult. The courts have established that Romany Gypsies, Scottish Gypsies and Irish Travellers are ethnic groups for the purposes of the Race Relations Act 1976 (as amended by the Race Relations (Amendment) Act 2000) (Commission for Racial Equality v Dutton, 1989; McLennan hearing October 2008, and O'Leary and others v Punch Retail, 2000). In Chapman v United Kingdom (2001) it was found that a person's occupation of their caravan is part of their ethnic identity. Previously, the focus has been on the nomadism of Gypsies and Travellers, as part of any legal definition for planning cases. However, the Department for Communities and Local Government (CLG), recognised the difficulties around the concept of 'settled' Travellers for housing purposes; it included the concept in Circular 1/2006 and in Statutory Instrument No. 3190 (2006). There are a number of different Gypsy and Traveller groups and cultures but this chapter will refer generally to Gypsies and Travellers when discussing issues that affect the wider travelling communities.

All counts of Gypsies and Travellers are estimates and there is no exact calculation of how many of them live in England, or indeed in Europe. The Department for Communities and Local Government (CLG) oversees a national bi-annual count of Gypsy and Traveller caravans, but this data is still not accurate. Nevertheless, until all Gypsy Traveller Accommodation Assessments (GTAAs) have been completed and figures compiled nationally, the CLG Count data suggests that in July 2008 there were 17,626 caravans of which 6,553 were on local authority sites, 7,083 on authorised private sites, 2,240 on unauthorised developments and 1,750 on unauthorised encampments. This disjuncture between the number of sites and the estimated population numbers and the numbers of caravans on unauthorised sites demonstrates the continued lack of resources and sites for Gypsies and Travellers in England.

Gypsies and Travellers continue to face discrimination and harassment in England. Despite the fact that for more than thirty years legislation has been in place to tackle discrimination on the grounds of race, this does not seem to have had the same impact for Gypsies and Travellers as for some other ethnic minority groups. Extreme political parties are partly responsible for the discrimination and harassment but so too are the media, politicians from the mainstream parties, and the general public. Trevor Phillips, Chair of the Commission for Racial Equality (now subsumed in the Equalities and Human Rights Commission) said at the launch of their draft Gypsy and Traveller Strategy in October 2003:

> For this group, Great Britain is still like the American Deep South for black people in the 1950s. Extreme levels of public hostility exist in relation to Gypsies and Travellers – fuelled in part by irresponsible media reporting of the kind that would be met with outrage if it was targeted at any other ethnic group. (Phillips, quoted in Crawley, 2004:2)

There are also issues of inequality in health, access to education and employment with the wider population. Parry *et al* (2004) state that:

There is now little doubt that health inequality between the observed Gypsy Traveller population in England and their non-Gypsy counterparts is striking, even when compared with other socially deprived or excluded groups and with other ethnic minorities. (p2)

This health study, and other reports, highlights that Gypsies and Travellers face increased infant mortality, lower life expectancy and difficulty in accessing health care. There is also a significantly higher chance of long term illness:

The scale of health inequality between the study population and the UK general population is large. There was more than twice the prevalence of limiting long-term illness and significantly poorer reported health in Gypsy Travellers. (*ibid*, p65)

Issues around education and the travelling population are discussed in CLG's (2006) *Improving Opportunity, Strengthening Society,* which notes that 'Gypsy, Roma and Traveller pupils have the lowest attainment levels of any ethnic group' (p15). These social inequalities are an important underlying concern in considering overall service provision and responses to Gypsies and Travellers.

Racism against Gypsies and Travellers

The murder of Johnny Delaney, a Traveller boy in Cheshire, in 2003 exemplifies the seriousness of the racism faced by Gypsies and Travellers: the discursive control goes beyond racist labelling by the media and others. He was allegedly kicked and beaten by other boys and called derogatory names because he was a Traveller.

A MORI poll undertaken on behalf of Stonewall in 2003 examined 'profiles of prejudice' (Valentine and McDonald, 2004). Sixty four per cent of respondents to the poll said that they were prejudiced against one or more groups. Of those, 14 per cent expressed a specific prejudice against Gypsies and Travellers: this was the highest figure, marginally above refugees and asylum seekers. In analysing this result, the report said:

Like asylum seekers these groups attracted openly prejudiced comments, indeed asylum seekers were often labelled 'gypos' and 'tramps'. Prejudices towards travellers and Gypsies were expressed in economic terms. It was argued that these groups did not conform to the system by paying taxes, they had a reputation for unreliable business practices and they did not respect private property.

They were also criticised in cultural terms for not belonging to a community and allegedly having a negative impact on the environment: for example, they are unsightly, dirty or unhygienic. A clear distinction was also made between Romany Gypsies, respected for their history and culture, and travellers or modern Gypsies. (Valentine and McDonald, 2004:12)

The perceived disjuncture between 'real' and 'fake' Gypsies and Travellers made by the settled community only isolates them further and provides the excuse for them to participate in, or acquiesce to, racist discourse and treatment of the travelling community as a whole (Richardson, 2006). There is also a challenge to the settled community to accept Gypsies and Travellers for who they are, rather than trying to assimilate them into a settled culture. Traditionally, this is where the tension between the state and travelling communities has occurred. Hawes and Perez (1996) sum up the situation between the state and the Gypsy/Traveller; they note the element of coercion to assimilate to a 'house-dwelling' norm: 'As one Traveller said, it is as if the *Gorgio* (non-Gypsy) is saying:

> Of course we must cater for your interesting differences, but we must encourage you, to the point of coercion, to stop being different – or at least make it as difficult as possible. (Hawes and Perez, 1996: 156)

Gypsies and Travellers are marginalised by a range of individuals and groups across the country: this includes local politicians, the media and members of the settled community. Coxhead (2007) examines the notion of 'identity and hierarchy in his research on prejudice and the policing of Gypsies and Travellers:

> One significant way that Gypsy identity is pushed to the bottom of the power hierarchy is through denying the existence of racism. One justice worker asserted that it was vital 'not to lose sight it's a race issue – we need to influence practitioners out there'. One reason for the non-recognition of Gypsies and Travellers was a blurring of white European ethnicity. As one Gypsy explained, 'the figures are buried in white European ethnicity, it's not seen as racism'. (Coxhead, 2007:62)

The issue of conflict between the settled community and Gypsies and Travellers is heightened in rural areas. Research has shown that because of isolation, the impact of racism and discrimination can be felt disproportionately by ethnic minority communities including Gypsies and Travellers in rural areas (Dialog, 2003).

Dhalech (1999) discussed the difference in the expression of racism in urban and rural areas. He suggested that in rural areas there was a predominant 'no problem here' approach to the issue, which was itself a major problem. Jay's

(1992) study highlighted the racism faced by ethnic minority communities in south west rural areas and also found the 'no problem here' syndrome in operation. Rural communities in 2007 (fifteen years after Jay's report) are becoming more diverse in their ethnic profile through new economic migrant communities working in agriculture and living in rural areas; and through Gypsies and Irish Travellers now being recognised under race relations legislation, so that discrimination against them can be recognised as racism.

Both Jay and Dhalech's reports are still important when examining community cohesion in rural areas, and some of the problems highlighted in the South West are equally relevant in other parts of the country. First the reports deal with racism, which is a term that has severe connotations for the perpetrator and the victim. This severity can get lost in generic terms such as 'community cohesion'. Second, Jay (1992) starts to explore one of the motives behind rural racism, this is developed further on in this chapter. He quotes one local government officer's warning about attitudes in Cornwall:

> It is fair to alert you to the fact that there is a substantial number of indigenous Cornish people who feel themselves disadvantaged compared with 'incomers' in relation to class, income, housing, employment and various other aspects of daily living. This manifests itself in a number of ways – for example, a feeling of 'losing out' to incomers in the scramble for affordable housing or the search for adequately remunerated employment, as well as concern about the erosion of traditional Cornish values and communities. (Jay, 1992:10)

The issue of scarce resources, particularly housing and employment, in changing rural economies seems often to be cited as a reason for racism and discrimination. An example of this rationale is cited in the IPPR (2007) report in relation to migrant workers:

> More negative views emerged over the perceived impacts of new migrants on local housing markets and the private rental sector. These were expressed across all social groups and centred on the affordability and availability of housing and rented property, which were widely believed to be reducing as new migrants move into the area. (IPPR, 2007:20)

This issue of fairness in the allocation of resources is also picked up in the report of the Commission on Integration and Cohesion in its *Our Shared Future* publication (2006):

> A new issue that we need to address is that settled communities are worried about the fair allocation of public services – with some thinking immigrants and minorities are getting special treatment. (Commission on Integration and Cohesion, 2006:9)

This is not a particularly new issue; the Jay report (1992) outlined a similar view from settled communities. Perhaps the numbers of new economic migrants in some rural areas and the physical presence of their 'otherness', Polish delicatessens, dual language signs in some shops and offices, a requirement for factory managers to speak Lithuanian or Polish all serve to highlight differences and 'newness' of some communities. The ensuing issue of 'fairness' and recognising long service to a community impacts heavily on new economic migrants. It also impacts on perceived new and different groups, such as Gypsies and Travellers, who have often been in an area for generations, much as land-owning members of the farming community might have been. In spite of their strong connections, Gypsies and Travellers are perceived to be new in some rural communities because of a lack of physical or social capital.

The difficulty lies in highlighting Gypsy and Traveller connectedness and belonging to a particular area, without highlighting the newness of other ethnic minority communities and perpetuating a divisive culture. Gypsies and Travellers and the settled community may share the concerns about new European migrants taking jobs and housing from longer standing residents. However, Gypsies and Travellers themselves are not even recognised as being resident by the settled community, even when they may have been living and working side by side for generations.

The lack of physical residence for Gypsies and Travellers is both the cause and effect of the conflict between local communities. Public debate over proposals for new Gypsy and Traveller sites provoke adverse and racist reactions from the local community, the media and politicians (Richardson, 2007). Some councillors, both at public meetings and in the local paper, have made highly inflammatory remarks which can only serve to stoke local conflict and little is done to stop or reprimand them. One example of this was in a rural district in the east of England:

> Mrs X had told fellow councillors that X District Council would 'never get rid of the b******' who had created an infamous illegal settlement ... The independent councillor ... declared: 'If I had cancer, I'd strap a big bomb around myself and go in tomorrow'. (*Daily Mail*, 24/01/07, p 35)

Holloway (2007) analyses in some depth a different incident in another rural area where, in 2003, a caravan with effigies of Gypsies was burnt as part of a bonfire night display. The reactions to the event and the subsequent reports were mixed and Holloway (2007) discusses the interesting phenomenon of people denying that Gypsies and Travellers are a racial group, or are in any way different. However, if they were not different then there would be less hostility to them settling in communities. This notion of difference which is adapted to suit all those voicing racist opinions is interesting. In his book *Multiculturalism*, Modood (2007) says:

> To speak of 'difference' rather than 'culture' as the sociological starting point is to recognise that the difference in question is not just constituted from the 'inside', from the side of a minority culture, but also from the outside, from the representations and treatment of the minorities in question. (Modood, 2007:39)

In much the same way that the debate on disability has moved from a medical model to a social model, which recognises the barriers that society places on the individual, rather than the restrictions caused by a particular medical condition, so the debate on difference concerning race and culture must recognise that difference can be a social construct that those issues and characteristics which make Gypsies and Travellers 'different' are small compared with all the issues which make them the same as other settled community members. It is the focus on, or the construction of the 'difference' which exacerbates the excluding and sometimes racist discourse in newspapers and town halls.

This discourse of difference and exclusion is particularly heightened during periods of consultation on new site provision, or following a particularly contentious unauthorised encampment, as in the quote from the councillor above. Language has been used by local authority officers in planning meetings that would be seen as racist if it were used about any other ethnic minority group. A particular issue seems to have arisen following publication of Gypsy and Traveller Accommodation Assessments (GTAA) and in debates at Examinations in Public of Regional Spatial Strategies. Numbers of new pitches required to meet the accommodation needs of Gypsies and Travellers are haggled over by local authorities and in some cases the numbers are reduced by re-examining assumptions in final GTAAs, under pressure from the local authorities. When the GTAA pitch requirements are then discussed in a regional Examination in Public, the numbers are further scrutinised by local authority planners in a debate on 'need where it arises' versus 'need where it should be met'. In some areas, this debate may well be down to the honest intention of a local authority to meet accommodation need where it will best suit Gypsies and Travellers.

However, in other areas it seems to be a debate on quotas and fair shares. At one Examination in Public one local district council complained that the sub-regional GTAA had found that one pitch was required in their area. Another district in the same region understood that there was a relatively high level of need coming out of the GTAA for their area, but wanted to share the provision of new pitches more widely in the region. This was because of a perceived level of unfairness in having more than their fair share of Gypsies and Travellers. It would simply not be acceptable for a local authority, in a strategic planning meeting on the provision of accommodation to say about any other ethnic minority group 'we have enough already, the burden should be shared'.

Unless positive action is taken, the cycle of this marginalisation of Gypsies and Travellers will persist. This means that there is continued hostility towards the travelling community: there is reluctance to back the provision of more sites, they continue to be moved on from place to place and are seen as outside the mainstream depictions of community and are 'other'. It has been highlighted that 'newcomers' are discriminated against in rural communities. Gypsies and Travellers are not newcomers – they have just not been allowed to settle in places they have lived and worked in for generations. It is important to break this cycle and to establish Gypsies and Travellers firmly as members of the community, not newcomers, in order to stop the discrimination and marginalisation.

Housing and government agencies have a role in breaking the cycle of conflict and racism. In the case of Connors, the European Court of Human Rights placed a responsibility on the UK government, to facilitate a Gypsy way of life and condemned the current policy regime:

> It would rather appear that the situation in England, as it had developed, for which the authorities had to take some responsibility, placed considerable obstacles in the way of gypsies pursuing an actively nomadic lifestyle while at the same time excluding from procedural protection those who decided to take up a more settled lifestyle. (European Court of Human Rights, 2004)

The Commissioner for Human Rights has also commented on the treatment of Gypsies and Travellers in the UK, particularly criticising the media:

> ...to judge by the levels of invective that can regularly be read in the national press, Gypsies would appear to be the last ethnic minority in respect of which openly racist views can still be acceptably expressed. (Gil-Robles, 2005:43)

Housing is a key agency in breaking the cycle of conflict and the discrimination which impacts on the lives of Gypsies and Travellers and in promoting greater tolerance. This is something that is echoed from the top of government. The minister clearly sees housing as a driving force for improved provision and greater community cohesion, as demonstrated by the drafting of the Housing 2004 duties to assess accommodation needs for Gypsies and Travellers and in Circular 1/06. The message from central government and the Local Government Association (2006) is that local authorities should be identifying need and developing new sites.

There is a political agenda which necessitates moving the Gypsy and Traveller site issue from conflict to consensus and cohesion; it is not possible to continue with the *status quo* in an area where there is tension over site provision. This political context for change includes human rights and race equality legislation, the sustainable communities agenda, social inclusion plans, as well as the political and academic debates on community cohesion. Fundamentally, the drive to move from conflict to cohesion is to allow the settled community and Gypsies and Travellers to be part of one community. Research for the Joseph Rowntree Foundation has examined the issue of managing and developing new Gypsy and Traveller sites, and found that many of the examples across the country are contentious; the report offers a framework of steps that can be taken to avoid or mitigate against conflict in planning for new sites (Richardson, 2007).

Legislation and government funding are backing a new era for housing associations and local authorities to get involved in site provision, which will be the first step towards showing that Gypsies and Travellers are a welcome part of the community, to enable better community cohesion and to defeat racism against the travelling communities.

Conclusion

The lack of residence for Gypsies and Travellers contributes significantly to fuelling social discord and to the racist treatment of travelling communities across Britain. The paucity of site provision meant that Gypsies and Travellers could not live according to their cultural norms. Approximately two-thirds of Gypsies and Travellers live in housing but when questioned in surveys, respondents talk about feeling trapped and isolated from their extended family and culture. Those refusing to accept accommodation and who cannot access local authority sites, or cannot afford to buy their own land and obtain planning permission, are faced with a life of living on the road and suffering constant eviction from place to place, sometimes three or four times a day. This is not multiculturalism at work but a process of forced assimilation into house-dwelling, or being made to face harassment and eviction.

Gypsies and Travellers are seen to be 'other' in society. Their difference in culture and values needs instead to be celebrated and allowed to flourish so that a whole way of life is not lost. However the social construct in the media and public discourse of the difference of Gypsies and Travellers needs to be examined. There is an assumption that Gypsies and Travellers either need to live up to an idyllic notion of the 'real' Gypsy or they should assimilate to settled norms. There does not seem to be room for the reality of modern day Gypsy and Traveller culture in our so-called multicultural society.

The current discourse of 'community cohesion' should be challenged and the word 'racist' needs to be used in context. Racist behaviour by individuals and by agencies is being hidden in the catch-all label of community cohesion. The language of race discrimination needs to be used more in the context of understanding the treatment of Gypsies and Travellers in our society.

The social housing sector is a key agency in taking forward some of these issues through practical measures, such as new site provision to demonstrate the physicality of residence in communities, and through providing support for cohesive communities. In its swan song report (2007) the CRE (now EHRC) charged the government to set up programmes to help asylum seekers, refugees and Gypsies and Irish Travellers to get involved in local community work. Local authorities and housing associations will be key delivery agencies in achieving this objective. Gypsies and Travellers are already a part of our communities recognising that, and promoting good race relations is the next.

References

Acton, T (1974) *Gypsy Politics and Social Change*. London: Routledge and Kegan Paul

Acton, T (1994) Modernisation, moral panics and the Gypsies. *Sociology Review*, Vol 4 (1) September, pp24-28

Acton, T (2000) (ed) *Scholarship and the Gypsy Struggle: Commitment in Romani Studies*. Hertfordshire: University of Hertfordshire Press

Acton, T and Mundy, G (eds) (1997) *Romani culture and Gypsy identity*. Hertfordshire: University of Hertfordshire Press

Cantle, T (2005) *Community Cohesion, a new framework for race and diversity*. Basingstoke: Palgrave Macmillan

Clark, C and Greenfields, M (2006) *Here to Stay, The Gypsies and Travellers of Britain*. Hatfield: University of Hertfordshire Press

Commission for Racial Equality (2006) *Common Ground: Equality, good race relations and sites for Gypsies and Irish Travellers*. London: CRE

Commission for Racial Equality (2006) *Safe Communities Initiative, Working with Gypsies and Irish Travellers in Cottenham* www.cre.gov.uk

Commission on Integration and Cohesion (2007) *Our Shared Future*, www.integrationandcohesion.org.uk

Communities and Local Government (2006) *Improving Opportunity, Strengthening Society*. London: DCLG

Connors v The United Kingdom (2004) (application no. 66746/01), *Press release by the Registrar of the European Court of Human Rights* http://press.coe.int/cp/2004/267a(2004).htm (accessed on June 4 2004)

Coxhead, J (2007) *The Last Bastion of Racism*, Stoke on Trent: Trentham books

Crawley, H (2004) *Moving Forward, the provision of accommodation for Travellers and Gypsies*, London: Institute of Public Policy Research

CRE (nd) *Safe Communities Initiative, Contingency Planning in Firle* www.cre.gov.uk

Daily Mail (2007) An explosive remark, January 24, p 35

Dhalech, M (1999) *Challenging Racism in the Rural Idyll*, London: NACAB

Dialog (2003) *Race is relevant: Implementing race equality schemes in a rural/semi-rural context*, London: IDeA (summarised on Idea website http://www.idea-knowledge.gov.uk/idk/core/page.do?pageId=5145184)

Gil-Robles, A (2005) *Report by Mr Alvaro Gil-Robles, Commissioner for Human Rights, on his visit to the United Kingdom*, 2004 Strasbourg Council of Europe

Hancock, I (2002) *We are the Romani People*. Hatfield: University of Hertfordshire Press

Hawes, D and Perez, B (1996) *The Gypsy and the State 2nd Ed.* Bristol: Policy Press

Holloway, S (2007) Burning issues: Whiteness, rurality and the politics of difference in *Geoforum* Volume 38 Issue 1, pp7-20

Institute of Public Policy Research (2007) *The reception and integration of new migrant communities*. London: IPPR

Jay, E (1992) *Keep Them in Birmingham Challenging racism in south-west England*. London: CRE

Kenrick, D and Clark, C (1999) *Moving On, The Gypsies and Travellers of Britain*. Hatfield: University of Hertfordshire Press

Local Government Association (2006) *Report of the LGA Gypsy and Traveller Task Group*. London: LGA

Mayall, D (1995) *English Gypsies and State Policies*. Hatfield: University of Hertfordshire Press

Modood, T (2007) *Multiculturalism*. Cambridge: Polity Press

Parry, G; Van Cleemput, P; Peters, J; Moore, J; Walters, S; Thomas, K and Cooper, C (2004) *The Health Status of Gypsies and Travellers in England*. Sheffield: University of Sheffield

Richardson, J (2006) *The Gypsy Debate: can discourse control?* Exeter: Imprint Academic

Richardson, J (2006) Talking about Gypsies: the use of discourse as control. *Housing Studies* Vol 21 No. 1, pp77-97

Richardson, J (2007) *Providing Gypsy and Traveller Sites Contentious Spaces*. Coventry: CIH/JRF

Valentine, G and McDonald, I (2004) *Understanding Prejudice, Attitudes towards minorities*. London: Stonewall

12

Community cohesion, the 'death of multiculturalism' and work with young people

Paul Thomas

The 2001 disturbances – a policy watershed

It is beyond dispute that the urban disturbances in northern England which occurred in the summer of 2001 have proved to be a watershed in the history of race relations in the UK (Solomos, 2003). Violent clashes between young Asian men and the police took place in Oldham in late May, Burnley in June and Bradford in early July 2001, with apparently racist young white men also a factor in Oldham and Burnley. A government-sponsored enquiry (Cantle, 2001) saw a common problem underpinning all three sets of disturbances, a lack of community cohesion, and a reality of stark physical and cultural segregation along ethnic lines. Whilst the locally-produced reports in Oldham and Burnley (Ritchie, 2001; Clarke, 2001) did not use the term community cohesion, they identified 'parallel lives' in their towns, implicitly accepting the government's analysis that ethnic segregation was partially responsible for the disturbances.

Bradford's report, commissioned before but published after the 2001 disturbances, painted a grim picture of all communities choosing to live apart (Ouseley, 2001). The lack of focus on the actual triggers to, and events of the violent disturbances in all these reports was in stark contrast to the previous watershed report into the 1981 Brixton disturbances (Scarman, 1981). This suggested that for the New Labour government these disturbances were symptomatic of deeper problems already acknowledged, namely that

Britain's apparent multiculturalism was superficial (CFMEB, 2000). Indeed, the policy goal, as well as the apparently limited reality of multiculturalism was now seen as problematic, with influential figures blaming policies of multiculturalism for the hardening and deepening of ethnic segregation over the past 20 years (Cantle, 2005; Phillips, 2005).

These pronouncements, and the associated criticism of the separateness and insularity of ethnic minority communities, mean that community cohesion represents the 'death of multiculturalism' for some critics (Kundnani, 2002). This chapter discusses the meaning and focus of community cohesion in relation to multiculturalism, drawing on empirical evidence on the operationalisation of community cohesion in Oldham, one of the key sites of the 2001 disturbances, (Watson, 2000; Thomas, 2006; 2007).

The emergence of community cohesion

Although a virtually unknown term prior to 2001, community cohesion has quickly expanded from being the explanation for the 2001 disturbances to being the dominant paradigm within governmental approaches to race relations and ethnic tensions (Flint and Robinson, 2008). Advice has been given to all local authorities on how to encourage and measure community cohesion with performance data having a key focus in Best Value and other inspection and audit regimes for local government ((LGA, 2002; Home Office, 2007). Community cohesion is a key plank of central government's Race Equality and Diversity strategy and promoting cohesion is now a statutory duty for all maintained schools in England under the 2006 Education and Inspections Act (Home Office, 2005). Community cohesion is arguably vital to both 'preventing violent extremism' amongst Muslim young people and to the integration of the increasingly diverse new migrant communities spread across the UK ((DCLG, 2007a; DCLG, 2007b; Thomas, 2009). Despite this rapid and widespread deployment, community cohesion remains a controversial and highly contested term. Empirical data on how community cohesion is actually being understood and implemented on the ground is sparse (Kalra, 2002; Burnett, 2004; Flint and Robinson, 2008).

Community Cohesion: 'The death of multiculturalism'?

A number of key themes can be detected within the community cohesion and 'parallel lives' discourse developed by the national and local reports and taken up as policy by central government. The key theme is physical and cultural ethnic segregation, the idea of parallel lives, with little common dialogue or shared identity. This view is contested, particularly the implicit suggestion that this segregation is getting worse, when much of the empirical data suggests a more optimistic long-term picture (Cantle, 2001; Finney and Simpson, 2009).

Nevertheless, ethnic segregation is significant in many towns and cities, and the emergence of community cohesion may well represent a more overt acknowledgement and frustration with this. We see the problemitisation of bonding social capital – the belief that the disturbances have exposed a reality of inward-looking and insular monocultural communities who have little interest in, or empathy for, other ethnic communities (McGhee, 2003; Putnam, 2000). There is an urgent need to develop avenues for meaningful 'bridging social capital' which will enable dialogue and relationships across apparently rigid ethnic divides, thereby facilitating the development of shared values and priorities. The third theme is the focus on 'agency' within the maintenance and solidification of ethnic divides, the belief that individuals and communities have *chosen* to accept separate, 'parallel lives', shown by their housing, schooling and leisure decisions. This was expressed most starkly in the claim of 'self segregation' in the Bradford report (Ouseley, 2001).

Whilst other commentators have distanced themselves from the suggestion that choice caused ethnic segregation, it is certainly seen as part of a way forward (Cantle, 2005). This is arguably part of wider and consistent focus on 'agency' across New Labour social policy and their belief that government alone cannot guarantee social change and that individuals must play a role (Giddens, 1998; Greener, 2002; Levitas, 2005). This is a clear communitarian suggestion that past policy approaches have focused on the rights of different ethnic groups without stressing the necessary and balancing shared responsibilities of us all to build an open and cohesive community (Cantle, 2001; Etzioni, 1995). Underpinning all these themes is the claim that governmental policy approaches to race relations over the past 25 years have deepened and solidified the divides between different ethnic communities.

This analysis sees post-1981 policy as having essentialised and privileged separate ethnic communities, and their community leaders within those enclaves, through funding for ethnic-specific facilities and organisations, a belief shared by left-wing critics of community cohesion (Sivanandan, 2005; Cantle, 2005). This policy approach can be traced right back to the establishment of the Commission for Racial Equality in 1976, where the concept of promoting good race relations amongst different ethnic groups was downplayed in favour of equality for each separate ethnic group (Solomos, 2003; Cantle, 2005).

The associated demand that Asian communities in Oldham, Burnley and elsewhere show *a universal acceptance of the English language, and develop a greater acceptance of, and engagement with, the principal national institutions* (Cantle, 2001:19) is more controversial. At the same time Citizenship and English tests for new migrants, a renewed focus on sub-continental marriage links, and the continued translation of official documents into South Asian languages has been queried (DCLG, 2007b).This apparently partial focus on Asian communities and the harsh sentences for many of the young Asian men involved in the 2001 disturbances has led to the suggestion that community cohesion represents a lurch back to the coercive assimilationism of the 1950s and 60s (Solomos, 2003) and so to the 'death of multiculturalism' (Kundnani, 2002; Burnett, 2004).

Community cohesion represents the end of the policy of recognising and celebrating ethnic difference, an approach claimed as dominant since 1981 but which has actually been central to governmental approaches. In 1966 Home Secretary Roy Jenkins defined multiculturalism as: '*not as a flattening process of assimilationism but as equal opportunity, accompanied by cultural diversity in an atmosphere of mutual tolerance*' (quoted in Sivanandan, 2005:1). Negative understandings of the meaning of community cohesion are understandable, given the position taken by the Chair of the CRE, Trevor Phillips that Britain is 'sleepwalking into segregation' and that multiculturalism is to blame (Phillips, 2005). Phillips and the CRE contrasted multiculturalism with 'integration', characterising it as a policy approach that has essentialised separate ethnic identities and accepted physical divides, whereas 'integration' is clearly seen as a more politically acceptable way of expressing the community cohesion focus on the need to bring people together around common needs and identities (CRE, 2007). Such perspectives make it even more vital that debates around community cohesion draw on empirical data on how it is actually being understood and used.

Research evidence: making community cohesion work

Given the dearth of such empirical evidence around how community cohesion is understood and deployed on the ground, this chapter contributes to the debate by offering evidence from field research in Oldham. Over 30 youth workers at all levels of responsibility from both the statutory and voluntary sectors were interviewed using semi-structured approaches during 2005 and 2006. The focus was on their understanding of what community cohesion means and how it has affected their professional practice with young people. Young people were heavily involved in the 2001 disturbances so improved youth work opportunities were explicitly identified as a way of avoiding youth tension in the future (Denham, 2001). The inadequacy of resources for youth work in Oldham was criticised, and it was suggested that prior to 2001, youth workers had failed to engage with young people amongst whom racial tension was a real issue (Ritchie, 2001). Governmental policy agendas do not translate easily into changed professional practice on the ground, and the nature of youth work practice leaves room for re-interpretation and modification. This evidence reflects how youth workers in Oldham have interpreted, used and responded to community cohesion policies.

Evidence from this field research suggests that community cohesion has led to a modal shift in youth work policy and practice within agencies in Oldham (Thomas, 2006; 2007). This shift has been based on a shared acceptance amongst youth workers at all levels of responsibility of the community cohesion analysis of ethnic segregation, and of the negative impacts of this on individuals and communities. There was also an acceptance of the role of agency. It is clear that structural racism, including overtly racist practices by housing agencies, created physical segregation in Oldham (Kundnani, 2001; Kalra, 2002). Respondents identified agency as having hardened and normalised segregation, with respondents of all ethnic backgrounds being critical of their own ethnic communities rather than of 'others'.

The youth work response has been to prioritise meaningful direct contact between young people of different ethnic backgrounds in all possible situations. Youth Centres serving different ethnic backgrounds have been linked on a long-term basis, allowing programmes of activities that bring young people together regularly, using traditional youth work mediums of arts, sport, outdoor activities and trips. One-off events such as *Eid* celebrations and Christmas parties, and residential trips away from Oldham have been organised, including an annual residential week for young people selected from every high school in Oldham, all facilitated by youth workers. This direct contact work has bridged geographical turf divides between areas. It has involved integration of young people with disabilities, showing a holistic concern with cohesion and horizon-widening more than a limited concern about 'race'. Rather than focusing formally on issues of diversity or racism, these events are about fun and association, allowing young people of different backgrounds to get to know each other informally. They join enjoyable group activities where any learning is spontaneous but is actually taking place in a planned and controlled environment (Smith, 1982).

This work is *not* about the denial of difference – work with individual groups in their own community-based settings is a vital part of preparation for direct contact activity. Community cohesion has led youth work agencies in Oldham to make meaningful direct contact across ethnic lines part of everything they do with young people. This is supported by deliberate decisions to deploy youth work staff to work with young people of different ethnic backgrounds to offer role models of dialogue and contact across those boundaries. These decisions break with the pre-2001 youth work professional orthodoxy stemming from the interpretation and implementation of well-intentioned anti-racist policies (CRE, 1999).

Whilst the quality and depth of these new community cohesion youth work approaches is inevitably variable in a professional context where significant degrees of face-to-face work with young people is done by part-time, partially (at best) qualified staff (Moore, 2005), it is clear that the analysis of community cohesion is supported by youth workers in Oldham and that it has led to significant shifts in the priorities and assumptions of professional practice with young people.

Community cohesion as critical multiculturalism?

This new emphasis by youth workers in Oldham on 'meaningful direct contact' could be characterised as 'transversal politics' (Yuval-Davis, 1997). The creation of safe space for contact and dialogue between young people across ethnic divides makes 'rooting and shifting' possible. This fosters willingness to explore the perspectives and experiences of others because your own perspectives and experiences are being acknowledged and supported rather than negatively criticised and challenged. The most convincing examples offered by respondents of genuine dialogue and learning by young people across ethnic lines concerned informal situations: dialogue naturally developed amongst young people at a time and in a manner of their choosing. This is illustrated by Mary's account of the annual Fusion residential, which brings young people together from high schools across Oldham and Rochdale, and requires them to work in mixed teams:

> A lot of the discussions actually happened at night in dorms or in the bedrooms when they're together ... For instance, one of the (Muslim) young women was praying at night, so the other girls watched her pray and asked her really interesting questions about it. The fact was it was done at one o' clock in the morning, and they should have been in bed, but I didn't stop it because it was a really interesting piece of dialogue that was going on.

Here, creating safe and apparently informal space was crucial – young people were unlikely to respond positively to invitations to debate issues of 'race' and difference. This supports the 'contact theory', which suggests that contact across problematic divides such as race or ethnicity needs to be in groups, over a sustained period, and done so that participants control and understand the process (Cantle, 2005; Hewstone *et al*, 2007).

This helps to answer the charge that community cohesion represents a lurch back to 'assimilationism' (Kundnani, 2001). The post-2001 reports and later government strategy documents (Cantle, 2001; Home Office, 2005) identify a clear and continued commitment to race equality measures: the detailed implementation of the Race Relations (Amendment) Act 2000 and its far-reaching race equality impact assessments, the detailed focus on ethnic disadvantage within school improvement and social exclusion policy areas, and the continued focus on racial harassment and other forms of hate crime (McGhee, 2006). Community cohesion represents a questioning of the essentialising and privileging of ethnic identities that has underpinned policy approaches for the past 20 years and a concern with more complex, and possibly 'hybrid' forms of identity (Hall, 2000).

These concerns were echoed by respondents, with a clear divergence of opinion over whether community cohesion should be concerned solely with race or with wider and more complex forms of difference. Supporters of the latter highlighted both the levels of youth territorial violence within mono-cultural communities and the need to focus on common forms of economic disadvantage (SEU,1999; Kintrea *et al*, 2008).

Such ambivalence on the ground is not surprising, given the same ambivalences in national community cohesion strategies. Initial pilot action research work included work with travelling and settled communities and on tension between older and younger monocultural generations (Home Office, 2003).The frequent slippage from community to social cohesion within such governmental documents can be seen as a deliberate attempt to avoid naming 'problematic' ethnic communities (Worley, 2005). It can also be seen as reflecting genuine ambivalence as to whether tension and segregation in poor, post-industrial towns like Oldham and Burnley can be fully explained through the prism of race and racism (Byrne, 1999). The attempt by government and by youth workers in Oldham to work with more complex understandings of youth identity through community cohesion can also be seen as consistent part of wider attempts to foster a multiplicity or 'intersectionality' of 'cooler' identities through a variety of governmental measures that have an overarching 'human rights' framework, rather than fixed, 'hot' ethnic/religious identities (McGhee, 2006).

Rather than representing a return to assimilationism, community cohesion has a more complex and nuanced relationship with multiculturalism. In both national policy and in the new local reality of youth work practice, difference, disadvantage and diversity are clearly recognised and worked with. Instead of being the 'death of multiculturalism', community cohesion arguably represents the re-thinking of a type of multiculturalism, namely what has been popularly known and understood as antiracism (Kundnani, 2002). This does not mean a rejection of the reality of structural racism, or the need to challenge racist actions and outcomes, but to revisit the policy approaches and assumptions that have been known as antiracism since the previous policy watershed of 1981. Here, there is evidence both of bad history and of a genuine disconnection between the way terms are used by academic writers and the way they are understood and used at a local level. Characterising multiculturalism as the policy approach which has essentialised and separated ethnic communities is highly questionable and does not reflect understanding on the ground (Phillips, 2005; CRE, 2007). Despite the misplaced claim that multiculturalism only emerged as a policy priority after the 1981 disturbances, it informed social policy approaches to ethnic minority communities, the development of anti-discriminatory legislation and education from the late 1960s onwards (Solomos, 2003; Bourne, 2007). For many progressive anti-racists, multiculturalism of this type was liberal and apolitical in its failure to face up to the realities of structural racism (Chauhan, 1990). There were growing demands for antiracist and equal opportunities policy measures in the wake of 1981. It was in the name of these policy approaches, rather than multiculturalism, that policy and funding measures that identified separate and specific ethnic groups for funding, facilities and consultation became the norm:

> This organic development of multiculturalism was to change when, in the early 1980s, the Thatcher government decided to actively promote cultural policies as a means of combating disaffection within minority ethnic communities. (Bourne, 2007:3)

There is some truth in this perspective but it underplays the extent to which this essentialising, antiracist version of multiculturalism was both called for and developed by progressive local authorities and ethnic minority community leaders (Solomos, 2003). This means that the multiculturalist policies of the 1980s and 1990s that were criticised by Trevor Phillips were actually carried out in the name of equal opportunities and antiracism. With blatant racial discrimination alive and well years after the implementation of the 1976 Race Relations Act, these policies were needed. There is clear evidence that these measures have had a significantly positive impact for many ethnic minority communities and individuals (Modood *et al*, 1997; Solomos, 2003).

However, there was also evidence that, in essentialising ethnic minority experiences, characterising all white people and communities as powerful and racist, these antiracist approaches could often be counter-productive in challenging the racist attitudes and behaviour that existed in Britain (Cohen, 1988; MacDonald, 1989; Bhavnani, 2001). In particular, antiracist educational approaches in schools and youth work often elicited a negative response from the white working-class young people it was aimed at and those attempting to work with them, such as youth workers (CRE, 1999; Hewitt, 2005). This negative understanding of antiracism was clearly evident in the Oldham field research, with respondents seeing its starting premise as negative, divisive and unhelpful (Thomas, 2007).The understandings of antiracism previously dominant within Oldham had prevented any work with young people across ethnic boundaries pre-2001 and educational approaches that were formal, didactic and off-putting.

An important distinction needs to be made here between opposing racism *per se* and the policy understandings and approaches of antiracism that had been developed and used in youth work and other arms of the public sector. Respondents were clearly opposed to racism and recognised its presence in Oldham and the need to challenge it; what they wanted to move on from, and which they saw community cohesion as helping them to do, was rigid, essentialising and prescriptive antiracism that does not reflect the complex realities of identity and experience on the ground.

So if community cohesion does represent the rejection or even death of multiculturalism, it is of a particular type of multiculturalism that needs to be called by its known name, antiracism (Kundnani, 2002; McGhee, 2006). This obviously poses a problem, which may explain why criticism focuses on multiculturalism rather than antiracism, How can a continued focus on opposing racism be ensured if the language and assumptions of antiracism are rejected? Whilst rejecting the policy approach of antiracism as out-dated and inappropriate, respondents recognised that opposing all forms of racism remains important and necessary, with some ethnic minority respondents expressing concern that community cohesion may represent a deflection from challenging racism through changing language and priorities. Some of the community cohesion youth work best practice described by respondents was about ensuring a continued focus on racism and prejudice within the creation of the conditions necessary for 'transversal politics' (Yuval Davis, 1997). The concept of 'critical multiculturalism' (May, 1999) is helpful, as it focuses on 'race' and ethnicity while avoiding reification or essentialism, so allowing more complex and contingent understandings of identity and experience to be focused on and worked with:

> Critical multiculturalism ... incorporates post-modern conceptions and analyses of culture and identity, while holding onto the possibility of an emancipatory politics. It specifically combines multicultural/anti-racist theoretical streams, which have, for far too long, 'talked past each other'. (May, 1999:7/8)

The best examples of community cohesion youth work practice in Oldham are at least creating conditions that make 'critical multiculturalist' approaches possible, in that ethnic differences are accepted but not taken as read, or seen as more important than other forms of identity.

Conclusion

As someone who was part of creating, shaping and implementing antiracist educational approaches with young people and communities throughout the 1980s and 1990s, I support the analysis that, whilst necessary and largely justifiable at the time, those policy approaches have become increasingly problematic in their reification and privileging of separate ethnic identities (Phillips, 2005; Cantle, 2005).Whilst not creating the problem of ethnic physical and cultural segregation in Britain's towns and cities – racism did that – policy approaches accepted and so hardened those ethnic divides, whilst also working with increasingly simplistic and out-dated understandings of identity and experience (Hall, 2000).

Characterising these policy approaches as multiculturalism seems to rewrite history as these policy approaches, ushered in by progressive local authorities in the wake of post-1981 reflections, were actually understood and used as a pursuit of antiracism and equal opportunities (Solomos, 2003). These approaches were explicitly seen as different from and an improvement on the apparently apolitical multiculturalist policies of the previous era (Chauhan, 1990). Whilst admittedly liberal, those multiculturalist policies did at least focus on dialogue and understanding across ethnic and cultural lines, and on promoting good race relations – something that became increasingly rare as antiracism became the norm, even as the problematic nature of much antiracist practice became more apparent (MacDonald, 1989; CRE, 1999; Hewitt, 2005; Cantle, 2005; Sivanandan, 2005).

This chapter has argued, on the basis of situated and contingent case study evidence from Oldham, that the post-2001 emergence of community cohesion as a new policy priority has provided the opportunity to move forward in productive directions. Community cohesion, though a slippery and problematic concept, seems to offer a way forward, with its focus on meaningful direct contact and dialogue across ethnic lines (Kalra, 2002; Flint and Robinson, 2008). The data gathered from field research with youth workers in Oldham highlights the positive understandings of this concept by youth workers, which is in dramatic contrast to their views on the meaning and implications of antiracism (Thomas, 2006; 2007).

Whilst inevitably contingent and patchy, the Community cohesion practice being developed seems to engage with more nuanced and complex understandings of identity within safe and informal dialogue, creating the potential for 'transversal politics' and the conditions required by 'contact theory' (Yuval-Davis, 1997; Hewstone *et al*, 2007). It also holds out the possibility of a more 'critical multiculturalism' (May, 1999) developing, which continues to acknowledge and work with the reality of race and racism but does not essentialise or privilege ethnicity above other important creators and forms of identity. This suggests that community cohesion is not the death *per se* of multiculturalism, but a moving on from antiracism or political multiculturalism towards a more nuanced version which represents a new and potentially fruitful phase of multiculturalism.

References

Bhavnani, R (2001) *Rethinking interventions in racism*. Stoke-on Trent: Trentham Books

Bourne, J (2007) *In defence of Multiculturalism: IRR Briefing Paper no. 2*. London: IRR

Burnett, J (2004) 'Community, Cohesion and the state'. *Race and Class* 45:3 pp1-18

Byrne, D (1999) *Social Exclusion*. Oxford: Blackwell

Cantle, T (2001) *Community Cohesion: A Report of the Independent Review Team*. London: Home Office

Cantle, T (2005) *Community Cohesion: A new Framework for Race Relations*. Basingstoke; Palgrave

CFMEB (2000) *The Commission on the Future of Multi-Ethnic Britain* (The Parekh Report). London: Runnymede Trust

Chauhan, V (1990) *Beyond Steel Bands 'n' Samosas'*. Leicester: National Youth Bureau

Clarke, T (2001) *Burnley Task Force report on the disturbances in June 2001*. Burnley Borough Council: Burnley

Cohen, P (1988) The perversions of inheritance in P Cohen and HS Bains (eds) *Multi-Racist Britain*. London: Macmillan

Commission for Racial Equality (1999) *Open Talk, Open Minds*. London: CRE

Commission for Racial Equality (2007) *Integration, Multiculturalism and the CRE* accessed via http://www.cre.gov.uk

Department for Communities and Local Government (2007a) *Preventing violent extremism: Winning hearts and minds.* London: DCLG

Department for Communities and Local Government (2007b) *Commission on Integration and Cohesion: Our Shared Future.* London: DCLG

Denham, J (2001) *Building Cohesive Communities – A Report of the Inter-Departmental Group on Public Order and Community Cohesion.* London: Home Office

Etzioni, A (1995) *The spirit of community: rights, responsibilities and the communitarian agenda.* London: Fontana

Finney, N and Simpson, L (2009) *Sleepwalking to Segregation? Challenging myths about race and migration.* Bristol: Policy Press

Flint, J and Robinson, D (2008) (eds) *Community Cohesion in Crisis?* Bristol: Policy Press

Giddens, A (1998) *The Third Way: the renewal of social democracy.* Cambridge: Polity

Greener, I (2002) Agency, social theory and social policy. *Critical Social Policy* Vol.22 (4) pp688-705

Hall, S (2000) Conclusion: The multicultural question in Hesse B (ed) *Un/Settled Multiculturalisms.* London: Zed Books

Hewitt, R (2005) *White Backlash: The Politics of Multiculturalism.* Cambridge: Cambridge University Press

Hewstone, M, Tausch, N , Hughes, J and Cairns, E (2007) Prejudice, Intergroup Contact and Identity: Do Neighbourhoods Matter? in M Wetherell, M Lafleche and R Berkley (eds) *Identity, Ethnic Diversity and Community Cohesion,* London: Sage

Home Office (2003) *Community Cohesion Pathfinder Programme: The first six months.* London: Home Office

Home Office (2005) *Improving Opportunity, Strengthening Society: The Government's Strategy to increase Race Equality and Community Cohesion.* London: Home Office

Home Office (2007) *Improving Opportunity, Strengthening Society: A 2 year review.* London: Home Office

Kalra, VS (2002) Extended View: Riots, Race and Reports: Denham, Cantle, Oldham and Burnley Inquiries, *Sage Race Relations Abstracts,* Vol. 27(4):pp20-30

Kintrea, K, Bannister, J, Pickering, J, Reid, M and Suzuki, N (2008) *Young People and territoriality in British Cities.* York: Joseph Rowntree Foundation

Kundnani, A (2001) From Oldham to Bradford: the violence of the violated in *The Three Faces of British Racism.* London: Institute of Race Relations

Kundnani, A (2002) *The Death of Multiculturalism.* London: Institute of Race Relations accessed via: http:///www.irr.org.uk/2002/april/ak000013.html

Levitas, R (2005) *The Inclusive Society?* (2nd edition). Basingstoke: Palgrave

Local Government Association (2002) *Guidance on Community Cohesion.* London: LGA

Macdonald, I (1989) *Murder in the playground – the report of the Macdonald Inquiry.* Manchester: Longsight Press

McGhee, D (2003) Moving to 'our' common ground – a critical examination of community cohesion discourse in twenty-first century Britain. *The Sociological Review* 51:3 pp366-404

McGhee, D (2006) The new Commission for Equality and Human Rights: Building Community Cohesion and revitalising citizenship in contemporary Britain. *Ethnopolitics* vol. 5:2 pp145-166

May, S (1999) Critical multiculturalism and cultural difference: Avoiding essentialism, in May, S (ed) *Critical Multiculturalism.* London: Falmer

Modood, T, Berthoud, R, Lakey, J, Nazroo, J Smith, P, Virdee, S and Beishon, S (1997) *Ethnic Minorities in Britain – Diversity and Disadvantage.* London: PSI

Moore, S (2005) The state of the Youth Service: Recruitment and Retention rates of Youth Workers in England. *Youth and Policy* no.88, pp29-44

Ouseley, H (2001) *Community Pride, Not Prejudice – Making Diversity Work in Bradford.* Bradford: Bradford Vision

Phillips, T (2005) After 7/7: Sleepwalking to segregation London: CRE, accessed via http://www.cre. gov.uk/default.aspx.LocID-Ohgnew07s.reflocID-OHG00900C002.Lang-EN.htm

Putnam, R (2000) *Bowling Alone – The Collapse and Revival of American Community.* London: Touchstone

Ritchie, D (2001) *Oldham Independent Review – On Oldham, One Future*, Government Office for the Northwest: Manchester

Robinson, D (2005) The search for Community Cohesion: key themes and dominant concepts of the public policy agenda. *Urban Studies* Vol.42 (8) pp1411-1427

Scarman, Lord (1981) *A Report into the Brixton Disturbances of 11/12th April 1981.* London; Home Office

Sivanandan, A (2005) I*t's anti-racism that was failed, not multiculturalism that failed.* London: Institute of Race Relations, accessed via http://www.irr.org.uk/2005/october/ak000021.html

Social Exclusion Unit (1999) *Bridging the Gap – New Opportunities for 16-18 year olds.* London: SEU

Solomos, J (2003) (3rd Edition) *Race and Racism in Britain*, Basingstoke: Palgrave

Thomas, P (2006) 'The impact of community cohesion on Youth Work: A case study from Oldham'. *Youth and Policy* no.93 pp41-60

Thomas, P (2007) Moving on from 'anti-racism'? Understandings of Community Cohesion held by Youth Workers. *Journal of Social Policy* 36:3 pp435-455

Thomas, P (2009) Between two stools? The Government's Preventing Violent Extremism agenda. *The Political Quarterly,* 80:2 pp282-291

Watson, CW (2000) *Multiculturalism.* Buckingham: Open University Press

Worley, C (2005) It's not about Race, it's about the community: New Labour and Community Cohesion. *Critical Social Policy* Vol.25 (4) pp483-496

Yuval-Davis, N (1997) Ethnicity, gender relations and multiculturalism in T Modood and P Werbner (eds) *Debating Cultural Hybridity.* London: Zed Books

Contributors

Tim Brown BSc (Hons), Dip TP, PhD, MCIH is Director of the Centre for Comparative Housing Research at De Montfort University. His main areas of expertise are housing market studies, choice-based lettings, community cohesion and rural policies. Current projects include a study on 'mixed communities' for the Institute of Community Cohesion and Black and Minority Ethnic Housing Issues in the East Midlands for the National Housing Federation. Tim is involved in consultancy and research for a wide range of organisations, including the Department for Communities and Local Government, the Joseph Rowntree Foundation, the East Midlands Regional Assembly and a large number of local authorities and housing associations.

Simon Dyson is Professor of Applied Sociology and Director of the Unit for the Social Study of Thalassaemia and Sickle Cell at De Montfort University, Leicester [http://www.tascunit.com]. He is the author of *Ethnicity and Screening for Sickle Cell and Thalassaemia* (Elsevier, 2005) and *Sickle Cell and Deaths in Custody* (Whiting and Birch, 2009), as well as numerous articles on the social and political aspects of sickle cell in such journals as *Critical Social Policy, Disability and Society, British Educational Research Journal* and the *Howard Journal of Criminal Justice*. He has worked for over 20 years with many of the voluntary groups for sickle cell (*Sickle Cell Society, OSCAR, Sickle Cell Disease Association of America, Sickle Cell Disease Association of Ontario*) and for thalassaemia (*UK Thalassaemia Society* and the *North of England Bone Marrow and Thalassaemia Association*).

Alan Grattan's main research interests include young people in conflict environments, political participation and social movements as well as issues relating to cultural identity and diversity. Alan is interested in issues relating to 'communities in conflict' and the processes of post conflict reconstruction and reconciliation. He was a member of the Youth Work in Contested Spaces Project which was a joint project between the University of Ulster, Youth Council for Northern Ireland and Public Achievement, researching and sharing ideas on working with young people in conflict and post conflict environments and is currently involved in research relating to youth and community development in Zambia. Previously he was a Junior Research Fellow at the Institute of Irish Studies at the Queen's University, Belfast, taught Sociology and Irish Studies at St. Mary's University College, Twickenham, UK and Community Studies at the University of

Ulster. He is now a lecturer in youth work and development in the Faculty of Law, Arts and Social Sciences at the University of Southampton, UK.

Carlton Howson has worked within the field of youth and community work for over twenty years, he has worked as a detached youth and community worker within the Belgrave area of Leicester as well as a race relations training officer for Leicester Social Services. He has also been a training advisor for youth workers and has undertaken a number of roles in which he has sought to support Black learners: including study supervisor and, Access Development Officer. He was the first Chair of the Black Prisoner Support Project. He was Chair of the Imani Ujima Centre, a project working primarily with the African and Caribbean community in Leicester. He has a keen interest in research and practice and uses education as a means of supporting others he has worked with at De Montfort University since 1990, as a senior lecturer. His main teaching areas are in social policy, sociology, Black perspectives and managing race and diversity. He has undertaken research in the growth of violence with weapons in Nottingham. In June 2006 he jointly organised a national conference *Working with Black Young People.*

Mark R D Johnson is Professor of Diversity in Health and Social Care and director of the Mary Seacole Research Centre at De Montfort University, Leicester. He is Clinical Lead of the NHS Specialist Library for Ethnicity and Health, to help staff in the NHS and social care access 'best available' evidence affecting the provision of care to a multi-ethnic population. (www.library.nhs.uk/ethnicity). He is also editor of the international journal *Diversity in Health and Social Care* (http://www. radcliffe-oxford.com/dhsc), and has thirty years experience of research into inequalities in health and the provision of services for a diverse, multi-ethnic society.

Martin McMullan works as assistant Director for Youth Work Strategy in Youth Action, Northern Ireland and has a proactive role in devising strategic plans and actions which engage particularly marginalised and under-supported young people. This has included staff training, funding applications, representation on strategic forums, writing articles, facilitating sector seminars, writing agency policy responses, involvement in European conferences, seminars and exchanges and creating partnerships with other organisations working with marginalised young people. He is involved in various European initiatives including the Western Balkans and the Baltic countries. His current post in YouthAction, Northern Ireland, is to support the development of the organisation's Youth Work Strategy. He is currently undertaking his PhD with the University of Southampton based on global influences on community identities in Northern Ireland.

Katrine Bang Nielsen completed her Masters at the University of Sussex, UK. She was employed as a researcher at the University of Sheffield on the Post-conflict Identities project about the experiences of young Somali refugee and asylum seekers between 2005-2007. She is currently an independent scholar based in Denmark

Jenny Phillimore is a Lecturer at the Institute of Applied Social Sciences at the University of Birmingham. She has been researching new migration for ten years, and has led a number of major projects in this area. These include a major EU funded project looking at the ways in which refugees' skills and experience can be accredited and documented, the JRF funded *Making a Difference project*, looking at the ways in which Refugee Community Organisations can use evidence to influence policy and projects for the Home Office, Learning and Skills Councils, Local Authorities, ESRC and other funders. She has written many reports for local, regional and national government on new migration, integration, employability and housing and articles for a wide range of journals including *Journal of Refugee Studies, Urban Studies, Journal of Inclusive Education* and *Social Policy and Society.* Her book, co-authored with Dr Lisa Goodson, *New migrants in the UK: education, training, employment, policy and practice* was published by Trentham in 2008. Their new book *Community research: from theory to method* will be published by Policy Press in April 2010. Dr Phillimore was a member of the NRIF and the employment and training sub-group

Tariq Ramadan is Professor of Islamic Studies. He is currently Senior Research Fellow St Antony's College, (Oxford), Doshisha University, (Kyoto, Japan) and at the Lokahi Foundation, (London). He is Visiting Professor (in charge of the chair: *Identity and Citizenship*) at Erasmus University in the Netherlands (www.eur.nl/fsw/ ramadan). Through his writing and lectures he has contributed substantially to the debate on the issues of Muslims in the West and Islamic revival in the Muslim world. He is active both at the academic and grassroots levels; lecturing extensively throughout the world on social justice and dialogue between civilisations and is currently President of the European think tank: European Muslim Network (EMN) in Brussels.

Jo Richardson is Principal Lecturer in Housing, in the Department of Public Policy at De Montfort University. Her area of research is Gypsies and Travellers, with a particularly focus on a discourse analysis. (She has recently published a book *The Gypsy Debate: can discourse control?*) and a number of chapters and papers. She has completed a research project for the Joseph Rowntree Foundation entitled *Providing Gypsy and Traveller Sites: Contentious spaces*, published in 2007. Jo is also increasingly looking at the shared challenges faced by the Gypsy/Traveller communities and new European economic migrants, particularly from A8 countries.

Momodou Sallah is Senior Lecturer at the Youth and Community Division, De Montfort University. He has over fifteen years experience working with young people at the local, national and international levels. He has a number of publications in the field of work with Black young people, young Muslims and globalisation/global youth work. His research interests include diversity, participation and globalisation in relation especially to young people.

Deborah Sporton is Senior Lecturer in the Department of Geography, University of Sheffield. She has long-standing research interests in the area of minority ethnic groups and migration and is currently a principal investigator (with Prof Gill Valentine, Leeds) on an ESRC funded project that is investigating post-conflict identities: *Practices and affiliations of Somali refugee children.*

Perry Stanislas is a Senior Lecturer at De Montfort University, Leicester, and teaches policing and applied criminology. His areas of research interest are international policing, policing diverse communities, and masculinity, ethnicity and violence. He received his PhD from the London School of Economics for his research on the leadership strategies of the Jewish, Hindu and African-Caribbean communities in influencing British Policing. His most recent publication is *The Cultural Politics of African-Caribbean and West African Families in Britain* (2009) in Hylton, C. and Oshien, B (ed) which examines the social changes which bring these communities in to contact with crime. Other work includes studies on ethnicity and violent homophobia in Jamaica and Britain. Dr Stanislas has nearly 30 years of practical policing experience working as a full-time policy advisor and consultant to British and foreign police services and other agencies involved in the areas of capacity building and crime prevention.

Paul Thomas is a Senior Lecturer in Youth and Community Work and Course Leader for the graduate-entry Youth Work programme at the University of Huddersfield, West Yorkshire, UK. He completed his PhD on *The impact of Community Cohesion on Youth Work* in Oldham, scene of violent disturbances in 2001. This research has led to journal articles in *Journal of Social Policy* (2007, 36:3) and Youth and Policy. Recently Paul has been carrying out research in Oldham and Rochdale, Greater Manchester in to young people's understandings of identity, and on the government's *Preventing Violent Extremism* policy agenda (*The Political Quarterly*, 2009, 80:2). Previously, Paul was North of England Regional Youth Campaigns and Policy Officer for the Commission for Racial Equality, worked with football fans in England and abroad around racism, and was a regional manager for a voluntary sector youth work organisation.

Gill Valentine is Professor of Geography and Director of the Leeds Social Science Institute at the University of Leeds. Her research interests include social identities, citizenship and belonging. She has held numerous academic and applied research grants, and is the (co)author/editor of fourteen books and over 100 articles. Gill's research has been recognised by the award of a Philip Leverhulme prize fellowship and the Royal Geographical Society's Gill Memorial award.

Marina Zhunich is a public affairs consultant focused on business diplomacy, corporate governance, civil society positioning, and stakeholders outreach. She worked in the Organisation for Security and Cooperation in Europe (OSCE) in Bosnia and Herzegovina where she fostered the establishment of a Youth Council in the formerly ethnically divided city of Mostar. Before that, she had been a correspondent and editor with the BBC in Russia and the UK.

Index

Also from Trentham

New Migrants in the UK
education, training and employment
Jenny Phillimore and Lisa Goodson

This study of the education, training and employment of asylum seekers and refugees in the UK is based on the academic and policy literature and empirical data from five major studies. It sets out the political context to seeking asylum in the UK, explores current policy and practice regarding the education, training andemployment of new migrants over the age of 16 and showshow policy affects their access to appropriate services.

The book draws on extensive empirical research to explore the education and training needs and aspirations of new migrants, their skills, qualifications and work experiences and how these relate to education, training and employment opportunities currently on offer in the UK. It also examines the perspectives of training providers and employers on working with new migrants. The authors conclude that the Government's laissez faire approach needs to be replaced with well targeted and resourced integration programmes that offer a model for practice.

With its combination of policy and literature analysis, up to the minute academic research and clearly presented policy recommendations, *New Migrants in the UK* will be invaluable to policymakers, academics and service providers.

Dr Jenny Phillimore undertakes research on the employability of new migrants and other excluded groups at the Centre for Urban and Regional Studies, University of Birmingham. Dr Lisa Goodson is a lecturer at the Centre for Urban and Regional Studies, specialising in qualitative methodologies and policy research in relation to new migrants.

2008, ISBN 978 1 85856 350 3
224 pages, 244 x 170mm
Price £18.99